Praise for the Nissim Ezekiel Centennial Volume

"The growing circle of Nissim Ezekiel's readers and admirers around the globe will find in this volume, brought together with love and care by Kavita Ezekiel Mendonca and Vinita Agrawal, an amazing gift, a treasure-trove of sight and sound evoked by poems, interviews, photographs, personal stories, and tributes. This centennial volume reminds us of the range of Nissim's appeal and complexity as a poet, public figure, critic, editor, teacher, mentor, friend, and family man. More than ever before, we can identify today with Ezekiel's India instead of Naipaul's and appreciate the "backward place" he chose to be part of. I can imagine Nissim receiving his copy in the other place—and finally tasting the "half a bite" he had craved for in that inimitable, impish short poem of his: "No, Lord,/not the fruit of action is my motive./But do you really mind half a bite of it?/It tastes so sweet,/and I'm so hungry."

– **Amritjit Singh, Langston Hughes Professor, Ohio University, author of *The Novels of the Harlem Renaissance***

"Poetry can act as a portal to the soul, transcending time and distance. Nissim Ezekiel is, for me, one of those great souls. His poetry, while steeped in Indianness, even Bombay-ness, far surpasses restrictive definitions such as 'an Indian poet'. His poetry is urgent and resonates with the quest of humans for meaning, love and intimacy, a quest he pursued with a well-honed and varied style, and with an empathic, humorous yet penetrating glance at the human condition. This centennial volume is a great tribute to a great poet. In not only reveals additional biographical facets of Ezekiel, but also demonstrates his enduring legacy by including poems written by his daughter Kavita and by many other poets, many of whom were supported by Ezekiel when starting their voyage"

– **Dr Gilad Jacobson, scientist, poet and Hebrew translator of Nissim Ezekiel's poems**

"The bittersweet flavors of remembrance, the wealth of personal and familial information (occasionally prompted by the need to set the biographical record straight), and the many tributes from poets, students, friends and family members, make this commemorative volume an important contribution to the knowledge and appreciation of Nissim Ezekiel. Of this poet who was also a husband and a father, a teacher, a mentor, an editor, a critic, and a public intellectual who shaped subsequent generations of Indian poets and writers, the book provides a complex and kaleidoscopic portrait, illustrating the various private and public dimensions of a man's life, while adding an important resource to the history of modern Indian poetry in English

– Dr. Graziano Krätli, Yale University, USA

"How does one write about a father who is an iconic figure in Indian poetry, a mentor to the next generation, and a person who showered love on a daughter he had named 'Kavita' - the epitome of poetry? Kavita Ezekiel Mendonca treads this complex ground with wisdom and sophistication as she creates a commemorative volume for Nissim Ezekiel's hundredth birth anniversary in 2024. Blending her personal narrative with the public fame of her father, Kavita presents a collection of memoirs, tributes, interviews and poetry - interspersed with photographs – that brilliantly offers archival material as well as a deeply moving story of genius and vulnerability. The recollections of poets such as Adil Jussawala, Gieve Patel and Sujatha Mathai carry the history of Indian poetry. And, when Nissim and Kavita Ezekiel's poems become interwoven as a fabric of togetherness, the colours are redolent with grace"

– Prof. Malashri Lal (retd., University of Delhi), Convener, English Advisory Board, Sahitya Akademi, India

"With every word soaked in the daughter's love for her father, Kavita Ezekiel Mendonca's commemorative volume could have

dwindled into becoming a sentimental bogie trudging on with the weight of a soggy narration, loaded with hyperbole. But instead, the restraint and the matter of fact style used by the writer creates a heartwarming intensity in her personal memoir of a father who came to be known as the doyen of Indian poetry in English. Kavita's deep connection with him unfolds itself in her poems as a rich poetic legacy left by Nissim Ezekiel. Yet, they are both beautifully 'alone together' in the book!"
– Sukrita Paul Kumar, poet & Editor of *Indian Literature*, the official journal of the Sahitya Akademi, India's national academy of literature

"Full of warm memories and thoughtful insights, this is a book to dip into and to mull over, one in which you catch glimpses of Nissim Ezekiel in many roles: the father, the mentor, the teacher and always, inescapably, the poet"
– Dr. Anna Kurian, Professor, University of Hyderabad, India

"If one wants to see a manifestation of deep love of a daughter for her father, it is Kavita Ezekiel Mendonca's assiduously-crafted commemorative volume. Filled with vignettes of family life, conversations, Nissim Ezekiel's life as a poet, and his interesting navigation between personal life and his writing told by his loving daughter, this celebratory volume offers us rare insights into the life of a great poet who is called the 'granddad of Indian English poetry'. Moreover, the father's humour, sometimes ironic, enters the memoir and keeps us hooked wanting to hear more stories about his life. Having experienced his humour, accompanied by his twinkling eyes, both when I was his student at Bombay University as well as in his poetry, I found myself chuckling through a good portion of the book and having flashbacks about my time in Ezekiel's classes and seeing the careful attention he gave to novice writers and translators. The interviews as well as the reflection of friends of Nissim Ezekiel support Kavita's own insights, thus allowing us a broad perspective shared by many who were fortunate to have met him and experienced his tutelage. Kavita is conscious about her father's influence on her poetry and at the same time finds her unique voice in some splendid poems such as 'Family Sunday', 'Give me Oil in My Lamp', 'sans punctuation', 'Bombay Fish Market', 'Loss', 'How Many Issues Do you Have?', 'How Daddy wrote his Poetry', and many more. Her poetry allows us a glimpse into the emotional life of the father and Kavita's inner world. Her description of her childhood home, aptly called 'The Retreat', is what Saleem Peeradina calls 'not just an ordinary address …, it was a place of historical interest', or even a fantastical land in the middle of an urban island. At the same time, Kavita's stories and poems about Nissim Ezekiel keep us grounded in the geography of Bombay, the history of Indian-English poetry publishing, the nature of family relationships when the patriarch chooses a profession that is out of the ordinary, details of Bene-Israel life in Bombay, and postcolonial experiences of establishing a uniquely Indian-English literature while having threads of connection to England and the U.S. What makes this volume precious are the photographs that accompany the memoir and poems, archival material that is not merely emotionally moving but is significant for researchers and future generations of Bene Israel Jews desiring to learn about their history"

– **Pramila Venkateswaran, Author of *We are Not a Museum* and of *The Singer of Alleppey*; Poet Laureate of Suffolk County, NY (2013-15); Professor, SUNY Nassau, USA**

"When it first appeared, Nissim Ezekiel's verse introduced a new realism into Indian poetry in English. A century after his birth, his voice remains as vital and enlivening as ever and it is a pleasure to see this fine volume, curated by his daughter Kavita, whose work is also included, keep the flame burning"

– **Professor John Thieme, author of the Introduction to the second edition of Nissim Ezekiel's *Collected Poems***

"How wonderful that Nissim lives on! There can be no history of postcolonial literature without him. There are those who define the path. He was one such light."

– **Yogesh Patel, MBE, Poet and Writer**

"In this seminal publication, a daughter's candour finds expression, through her love and understanding of a poet father whose entire life was given selflessly to poetry and to the encouragement of young, new aspiring poets. Nissim Ezekiel put modern Indian Poetry in English on the global map of poetry that was quintessentially Indian and could be distinguished for its unique voice and cadence. All subsequent poets from India, writing in English, owe a debt to Ezekiel for providing that niche for creative expression in the language of the one-time coloniser and claiming it as their own. Yet, the legacy Ezekiel left behind is colossal and difficult to acknowledge and do full justice to. And this is exactly what Kavita Ezekiel Mendonca has done in this commemorative volume, bringing together various voices who have been encouraged, supported and published by Ezekiel in the inimitable journal, Indian P.E.N., of which he was the editor, as evident in the many tributes paid by poets in this volume. The pieces by family members, friends and the extended family, enrich this book, showing how Ezekiel touched multiple lives. As Kavita says, her father was the poet and she the poem/poetry, a name he gave her at birth which was imbued with prophecy and expectation. Yet Ezekiel, with his characteristic sense of justice, did not mentor and tutor her poetry, though he was immensely proud of her work. Kavita's poetry flowed on the page with unbounded legitimacy. Her poetry, as she acknowledges, was either in answer to her father's work or intricately interwoven with his imagery. She calls these 'Tangential Poems', a sub-genre developed by her, in which a torch passed on by her father is held up and passed on like a baton to those who follow in Ezekiel's groundbreaking footsteps, from her Bombay roots, the Mussoorie hills and Canadian 'wildness'. Kavita's trajectory is like that of the shooting star. She glides across the firmament, noticeable and resplendent. The loneliness that comes with having to leave her mother and siblings, is a sensibility that remains with her, and 'Waiting for Daddy', becomes a refrain in her many vigils by the window, waiting for the step on the stair as he father enters at 11 pm, calling out affectionately to 'Kavitam!' The conversational tone of the poems, enhance their appeal and make this book accessible and memorable for the reader, in a commemorative volume that reaffirms Ezekiel's rich legacy"

– Dr Bashabi Fraser CBE, HonFASL, Professor Emerita of English and Creative Writing, Edinburgh Napier University; Director, Scottish Centre of Tagore Studies

"Lovingly put-together … a valuable addition to the larger archives of modern Indian poetry"

– Sudeep Sen, author of *Anthropocene* (Rabindranath Tagore Literary Prize winner)

NISSIM EZEKIEL, POET & FATHER:
A CENTENNIAL CELEBRATION
(1924 – 2024)

compiled by Kavita Ezekiel Mendonca
edited by Vinita Agrawal

Pippa Rann
books & media

Pippa Rann
books & media

An imprint of
Salt Desert Media Group Limited,
7 Mulgrave Chambers, 26 Mulgrave Rd,
Sutton SM2 6LE, England, UK.
Email: publisher@pipparannbooks.com
Website: www.pipparannbooks.com

ISBN 978-1913738-23-5

Printed and bound in India by Replika Press Pvt. Ltd.

MIX
Paper | Supporting
responsible forestry
FSC™ C016779

DEDICATION

Dedicated to my father, the late poet Nissim Ezekiel,
on the occasion of his Birth Centenary.

If I could pray, the gist of my
Demanding would be simply this:
Quietude. The ordered mind,
Erasure of the inner lie,
And only love in every kiss.
(Lines from 'Prayer I' by Nissim Ezekiel)

When eyes are open let me see,
Let words be intimate with brain
And let the road, the house or tree
Not sprawl across my life in vain.
(Lines from 'Prayer II' by Nissim Ezekiel)

CONTENTS

ACKNOWLEDGEMENTS

My sincere thanks go to the special people who helped in bringing the Centennial Volume to fruition: Vinita Agrawal for editing the book and writing the Introduction.

To my husband Alan for all his help, love and support, for spending. countless hours designing and formatting the book and reading the Memoir.

Thanks to Dr. Yudit Kornberg Greenberg for writing the Foreword.

Thanks are also due to the poets, writers, students, friends and family who so willingly shared their memories of my father and other contributions here.

Many thanks to Dr. Shalva Weil for permission to include several of her photographs in this book.

Gratitude to the editors of the various magazines who have published the poems included in the section 'The Daddy Poems' – A.J. Thomas, Ambika Ananth, Anita Nahal, Arindam Roy, Basudhara Roy, Candice Louisa Daquin, Dustin Pickering, Eliza Filimon, E. Ethelbert Miller, Feroza Jussawalla, Gopal Lahiri, Inam Hussain Begg Mullik, Jaydeep Sarangi, Jim Lewis, John Eliot, Linda Barone, Lopamudra Basu, Malashri Lal, Megha Sood, Nandini Sahu, Saudamini Deo, Shrenik Rao, Siddharth Sehgal, Steve Carr, Sudeep Sen, Sukrita Paul Kumar, Udayan Thakkar, Vinita Agrawal, and their associated editors, for work from these print periodicals and webzines: *Different Truths, Harbinger*

Asylum, Indian Periodical, Journal of Indian Literature in English, Madras Courier, Muse India, Poetry India, The Quiver Review, RIC Journal, Setu Magazine, Verse- Virtual, and Usawa Literary Journal; and the following books and anthologies: *Around The World Landscapes and Cityscapes* (2021), *Best Asian Poetry* (2022), *The Salerno Project (2022), Explorations in English Poetry (2021), The Kali Project* (2021), *Soul Spaces,* (2023), *Through the Looking Glass* (2020), *Yearbooks of Indian Poetry in English (2021, 2022, 2023), Silver Birch Press (Los Angeles, 2022), South Asian Women Write Trauma Forthcoming).*

My thanks to the respective interviewers for permission to print their interviews with me: Basudhara Roy and Jaydeep Sarangi ("Writers in Conversation" series, Flinders University, Australia, August 2020), Urna Bose (*Different Truths* magazine, 13 February 2021), Usha Kishore (*Muse India*, March-April 2021), and Yogesh Patel (*iGlobal News, 20* January 2022).

Gratitude to my publisher Prabhu Guptara for not only being thorough and professional, but for making the whole process of working on the book a pleasurable experience.

FOREWORD

Despite representing a miniscule component of India's population, its Jewish citizens have made significant contributions to India's culture and society. The recognition of Nissim Ezekiel's poetry as an inspiration in the sphere of creative literature is a prime example of this contribution. Others include Lt Gen JFR (Jack) Jacob, who was the highest-ranking military officer in the history of the Indian Jewish community and is considered an Indian national hero, as well as the Jewish actors and actresses (Sitaras) who played major roles in the early history of Bollywood cinema. And of course, David Sassoon and his descendants, whose legacy in the development of Mumbai is so visible in the city today.

Since first coming to India in 1993, I have considered India my second home after Israel and have continued to find emotional, intellectual, and spiritual connections there. While I did not have the opportunity to meet Mr. Ezekiel, I have encountered his work many times in my focus on Indo-Judaic studies and have always been deeply moved by his poetry.

I was privileged to receive two Fulbright-Nehru Scholar Awards which enabled me to live in two of the most vibrant cultural cities in India – New Delhi and Mumbai. In Mumbai, my husband and I participated in weekly Shabbat services at the Knesset Eliyahu Synagogue, as well as attending holiday events and celebrations at several of the city's Bene Israel synagogues.

Kavita's poem "Alibag" beautifully expresses the deep connection I felt with India's Jewish history on our visit to the town and its remaining synagogue, as well as the nearby site of the Rock of Eliyahu, where the prophet Eliyahu Hanavi is said to have stopped in his chariot of fire as he ascended to heaven. We were privileged to participate in a Malida ceremony, also known as a Seder Eliyahu Hanavi or "Giving Thanks" ceremony, which was performed to mark an engagement. This ceremony is a perfect example of the blending of Jewish ritual and traditional Hindu Aarti. Reflecting about the diverse contributions of Jews to India, I also want to acknowledge our good friends Col. Oliver Hyam (ret) who served 35 years in the Indian Army, and his wife Sheila Hyam Kolet, leading members of the Bene Israel community in Pune, who graciously shared their Shabbat with us.

While in Mumbai, I taught a graduate course in comparative religion at the University of Mumbai and the Somaya Institute of Buddhist Studies. During my five months stay, I also researched the history of Jewish movie stars in the early years of Bollywood. Referred to as Sitaras (starlets), they negotiated and constructed their identities as women, as Jews, as Indians and as actors. In an article published in the Association for Jewish Studies journal, I claim that the Jewish Sitaras had a pioneering and ground-breaking role as actresses in the burgeoning film industry, despite Indian patriarchal taboos against exposing women's bodies and women's social power. They exercised their agency and consequently legitimized female empowerment, on and off the Indian screen, challenging existing social taboos and contributing to the redefinition of gender roles in modern India.

My scholarship in Jewish Studies expanded over the years to include chairing the Hinduism and Judaisms section of the American Academy of Religion, as well as co-editing Dharma and Halacha: Comparative Studies in Hindu-Jewish Philosophy and Religion. (https://rowman.com/ISBN/9781498512794/ Dharma-and-Halacha-Comparative-Studies-in-Hindu-Jewish-

Philosophy-and-Religion). My work comparing the biblical Song of Songs and the Gita Govinda is featured in this volume, wherein I explore the parallels between the Hindu attachment to the land, flora, and fauna in India and the Jewish attachment to the Land of Israel. The Indian-born Jewish artist, Siona Benjamin, contributed her art to the cover of the book.

As one of the few places on earth where anti-Semitism has never flourished, it is truly an honor and an inspiration to offer congratulations to Kavita for assembling this tribute to her late father, and to see Nissim Ezekial and his expressive poetry praised and recognized. *Am Yisrael Chai Be-Hodu* – The people of Israel Live On – in India!

Yudit Kornberg Greenberg
12 February 2024

Dr Greenberg is The George D. and Harriet W. Cornell Endowed Chair of Religion, and the Founding Director of the Jewish Studies Program at Rollins College, Winter Park, Florida, USA.

She was Co-Chair of the Comparative Study of Hinduisms and Judaisms Group at the American Academy of Religion from 2004 to 2011. Among her many books is *Dharma and Halacha: Comparative Studies in Hindu-Jewish Philosophy and Religion.*

INTRODUCTION
Vinita Agrawal

A Patremoir of Love and Reflection

No matter how tall I grow, I still look up to you.

Just before a new session began at school and fresh textbooks had been bought, I would pick out the English Reader and read it front to back. In class X (in 1982) our English textbook contained Nissim Ezekiel's 'Night of the Scorpion'. I clearly remember reading it and being blown away by its imagery. To my tender, fifteen-year-old mind, it seemed as though I'd read something precious – something graphic and powerful. That was my first introduction to the poetry of Nissim Ezekiel. When classes began and Mrs. Kar, our English teacher, finally got around to teaching Nissim's poem, I recall clearly how mesmerized I was as she took us through those unforgettable lines.

Unfortunately, I could never meet Nissim in person. Could never have the opportunity to discover what he was like as an individual. However, I did read a lot of his poetry. He stood out for me as one of the founding pillars of Modern Indian Poetry in English. His works seemed to me to define the essential ethos of writing poetry in our country. It also spoke to my soul. I regret not having met him.

Which is why, when his daughter Kavita approached me to edit this memoir anthology, marking the centennial year of his birth, I readily accepted the proposal. It felt like a small redemption for not having met Nissim in person. Surely this was as close I as I was going to get to the man, to the poet, now that he was no more in our midst.   The actual experience of editing this deeply moving patremoir, compiled with admirable honesty by Kavita, was more than I'd bargained for. I imagined I'd get to know Nissim better through this manuscript but I hadn't anticipated the singular welling of emotion towards Kavita in the course of reading these pages. Kavita, who bared her deepest vulnerabilities in her recounting of her life with her father. The section where she narrates, how at the age of ten, when her parents had separated, her mother insisted that she go and live with her father and bundled her into a taxi, made me pause and take a deep breath. It couldn't have been easy to have no choice in the matter.

Kavita reveals more of her robbed childhood; about taking what she was given, or left with, and making the best of it. She does so with wisdom and restraint. Sometimes one has to read between the lines to gauge the true extent of her loneliness and how raw she must have felt on the inside. The kind of experiences she shares with the readers can make or break a person. For Kavita, the beautiful soul that she is, they helped her evolve into who she is today – a wholesome, mature woman without the destructive bitterness that comes with a difficult childhood. It's important to add here that her childhood was not short of love, just short of the *presence* of both parents.

A memoir requires perspective and insight in order to be beautifully portrayed. For every good Father Memoir, there are dozens of bad ones – published because of sensational material or because of too many details about Alzheimer's, or some such currently-popular subject for such memoirs. However in 'Waiting For Daddy,' the Alzheimer's that afflicted Nissim in the later stages of his life is not overplayed. It is simply the crease on the paper that folded up his life. A health issue. The reader is not subjected to any appalling details of that condition.

At the end of reading the manuscript, I was left with the sweet glow of Nissim's postcards to his daughters hoping that they'd both turn out to be marvellous writers like the Bronte sisters and the tremendous affection he garnered from his colleagues and students, friends and family, as is apparent from the dedications and essays contributed by a plethora of writers and friends especially for this book. The Father-Daughter genre is certainly not an empty field. Aminatta Forna's *The Devil that Danced on Water: A Daughter's Quest* is a well-known memoir among so many others. As are Father-Son memoirs, most notable amongst them being, perhaps, Kafka's *Letters to His Father*.

Memoirs are penned sometimes to clear the air in difficult relationships. Not this one. The purpose of this memoir is celebratory. It marks the glorious centennial of the year of Nissim's birth and affords his daughter, Kavita, to bring under one roof some of the people who knew him, alongside her own precious memories of her beloved father and the rest of the family's memories as well. There's much more to this memoir anthology than I can possibly summarize in a mere foreword. Suffice to say that it's a one-of-a-kind collection of memories and poems, essays and tributes to an Indian poet who wrote in English, lived life on his own terms and showed the way forward to many poets of the future generation. The exquisite thing about this anthology is that there are intersections of unforgettable emotions here and heartbreaking glimpses of what was beneath the surface as life unfolded in the Ezekiel family. Kavita has an exceptional ability to embed emotions in her descriptions. This book is anchored in the senses and at its heart is the love of a daughter for her father.

Finally, I'd like to say this – memoirs often record the psychological pressures of growing-up years. This one does too. But it does so with amazing courage and fortitude, poignancy and frankness, honesty and originality, making it a particularly rich and rewarding read. Kavita's quotes from her poems as she takes us through her journey with Nissim, add a layer of literary tapestry appropriate to a memoir dealing with a literary personality. In intertwining her father's story with her own, Kavita holds nothing back, leaving the reader marvelling at how much life exacts from mere mortals. Through it all Nissim emerges as a terrific literary figure, passionate about his writing, profoundly dedicated to art and literature, living an unpretentious life. He bequeathed his daughter a treasury of love and fondness and of course cherished creative skills. With Kavita, Nissim's legacies are in safe hands.

I applaud each and everyone who is a part of this book. Some for delving deep into their memories to bring their association with Nissim to the surface and others for paying tributes to him through poetic verses. Above all, I'd like to express heartfelt admiration for Kavita for telling us her story with unflinching honesty. And for shining the light on Nissim, again. It's only appropriate that in this, the 100th year of his birth, we get together and celebrate a great poet – his glories, his writing, his poetry, his journey.

I'm deeply grateful to be a part of this celebration, to be a part of a brilliantly compiled, loving testament. It's an opportunity I treasure with all my heart. To be alive is to be made of memories – and I cherish my small part in this expression of lived reality, a precious tribute to a living legend – Nissim Ezekiel.

Vinita Agrawal
Indore, India.

MEMOIR

Waiting for Daddy

A Memoir, purely a labor of love
with words straight from the heart.

Kavita Ezekiel Mendonca

It doesn't matter who my father was…
it's how I remember who he was.

Anne Sexton

'A legacy is every life you've ever touched' Maya Angelou

On December 16, 1924 in Bombay, Moses and Diana Ezekiel welcomed their third child into their family. They named him Nissim, which in Hebrew means miracle. It also carries the multiple meanings of sign, wonder, and blessing. He was perhaps destined to be my father Nissim Ezekiel, the man I would call daddy for the rest of my life. My favorite story about him was one my grandmother told me. She narrated how one day, at the age of five, he simply disappeared from the house. The family went door to door frantically searching all the seven bungalows of 'The Retreat' which was the name of their residence. He had boarded a tram, which was a mode of transport in the Bombay of those days, and of course he was lost! Fortunately, he knew the directions to his home and the kindly conductor of the tram dropped off the little boy at the gate to his home. His mother was right there waiting for him, and you can only imagine her joy. When questioned, Nissim told his mother that he had gone to purchase a suit like the one his father wore!

Was this the start of his love of adventure? I wonder.

> *A poet-rascal-clown was born,*
> *The frightened child who would not eat*
> *Or sleep, a boy of meagre bone*
> *He never learned to fly a kite,*
> *His borrowed top refused to spin.*
> ('Background Casually' Nissim Ezekiel)

Though this is a personal memoir, it is challenging to separate my father from the poet that he was, and I am tempted to narrate a story he told me about poetry, that was so central to his life. He said that there was some sort of writing competition in his school. He won a prize for a poem he had written. The prize was four *annas* (old Indian money, now discontinued), and he bought a bar of chocolate with the money. He went home, and with great excitement, told his father that he had won a poetry prize. "Poetry?", my grandfather said, "What's that?"

My father's whole life was an answer to that question; I have captured his imagined reaction as a young boy, to his father's words in my poem, 'How Daddy Wrote His Poetry':

> *Who ate his treat in solitary Silence*
> *And tears of wept Hurt*
> *Mingled with Hope*
> *And secret Determination*
> *To pursue the*
> *Poetic journey.*

The proverbial 'Time Flies' comes to mind when I try to wrap my mind around the fact that a hundred years have passed since my father was born, and the speed of the passing years. It is a time to celebrate the life and love of a father whose presence touched so many lives, more so especially mine, as his daughter, my name *Kavita*, creating the first bond with him.

> *He believed his daughter was a gift from his God*
> *She would be named *Kavita, symbolically.*
> (Lines from my poem 'The Poet's Breath.')
> (*Kavita means poem in Hindi)

I am certain my father did not name us on an impulse, rather he put much thought into our names. He named my sister Kalpana, which means imagination, my brother Elkana, which means gift of God, after a promise made to my father's very dear friend Ebrahim Alkazi, nicknamed Elk. My brother is now affectionately known by the name Elkie, close enough to Elk. My grandfather spoke Sanskrit and I wondered if my name and my sister's was influenced by this. The fact that my sister and I were given Indian names reflects my father's pride in his Indianness. He was Indian to his very core.

What a blessing to be welcomed into the world by a happy father, a man who held me in his arms when I took my first breaths, chose a name for me as something almost as an extension of himself, and celebrated my worth and value as a girl, when so many in India devalued girls.

> *A poet with a different philosophy*
> *Entered the room*
> *Listened to my first breaths*
> *Cradled me in his arms*
> *Breathed a name on me*
> *Speaking it quietly, almost a whisper*
> *Yet, loud enough for all to hear*
> *His joy would shower poems on her*
> *While others with girl-children*
> *Knit their brows, puzzled…*
> (Lines from my poem 'The Poet's Breath.')

I am equally humbled and proud not just to be his daughter, but in some small way to be the bearer of his precious legacy, and to share it with the world. 2024 is the 100th Birth Anniversary of my father. It is befitting to celebrate a kind, gentle, calm, funny, compassionate, caring, gracious and generous man, who loved life, and lived it in all its fullness. The adjectives I have chosen to describe him are not just well-worn ones, but loaded with meaning well beyond their dictionary definitions because of the selfless and philanthropic acts that are associated with his character and personality.

> *For everything there is a season,*
> *And a time for every purpose under heaven.*
> Ecclesiastes 3:1-8 American Standard Version

I look back and reflect upon that special time in my family's history with much gratitude – those myriad lessons of resilience, humility, can-do attitude, positive thinking, and integrity that he taught me. Lessons about living with a strong belief in using time well, the reminder to take seriously the words of Thoreau 'many live lives of quiet desperation', as an invocation to find one's purpose in life, discovering what it is you love in life, and then embracing it fully. Lessons that were always set by example, never dictating what must be done, and expecting compliance. Lessons about reaching out to those less fortunate than oneself, and always putting others before self. It is a special time to reflect on his great sense of calm that could take success and adversity in stride, his endless curiosity for learning about any and everything life had to offer, whether it was experimenting with LSD (an interview about this appeared in a leading Indian newspaper, much to the embarrassment of our family!), or going to meet Rajneesh to discover for himself what he was all about, even visiting a street horoscope reader, to learn what the future might hold for him. His selfless giving of his time and energy to mentor those who came to him for guidance and advice, whether it was in relation to poetry, or in the role of a personal counselor, was a rare quality, in those days, and especially today. No one was turned away. It did not matter how busy he was. He simply was a man made in a different mould. It would not be an exaggeration to say that my father dedicated his life to the service of the literary community in India. I was almost tempted to title my memoir '*The Man Who Never Said No*,' or '*Sharing Daddy*.'

When he was invited to join the American Joint Distribution Committee (Bombay Chapter) which is a leading global Jewish humanitarian organization and '*whose mission is quite simple – to care for the most vulnerable, develop innovative ways to fight poverty and build community with Jewish and non-Jewish people*', he was reluctant to take on the task because of his paucity of knowledge about finances. Ultimately he accepted the voluntary position and loved his work, because it was devoted to the needs of others.

His work at PEN India, in Bombay, to which he was completely dedicated, was also in a voluntary capacity. My father loved his work there and spent countless hours mentoring younger poets, surrounded by writers and shelves crowded with manuscripts. I would meet him there to have lunch with him, but would have to wait quietly at the door, waiting for my turn to enter his heart, as expressed in my poem, below.

Waiting for Daddy

Daddy, the poets have gone home now
They have taken their commas and full stops with them
You must be hungry now, daddy
Let's have lunch together,
I have brought along my poem
But it can wait,
I can wait.
Eat slowly, take your time, enjoy your meal
Let's laugh together
At those silly 'knock knock' jokes
You love to tell,
Don't worry about the clever student
Who will be waiting in the wings
To ask you questions about your life
And then ask others, who with masks of love
Rob a man of his private suffering
To indulge a world with its love of sensationalism.

You answer the questions about your poetry
You authorize the literary journey
Then your memory fades

You are not public property anymore, daddy
Private Property, no trespassing.

You took your answers to the grave
We were splashed with the mud
And they with false fame,
How little it mattered to them,
They who chose ignorance
Of how we waited for you
With our poems and our love
And how it broke our hearts...

He took the train from Bombay Central Station, a fifteen-minute walk from his home, to Churchgate each morning, and was at his desk at promptly nine a.m. After his cataract surgery and even in the throes of Alzheimer's, he insisted that he wanted to go to the PEN office. "I'm needed there," he would say. I wonder if he knew how much he was needed 'here,' where I waited patiently for him, in what seemed like a lifetime.

Nothing epitomizes waiting more
Than a boat on the shore
Or an urn of warm ashes
Tied to a tree or a clothesline
(From 'I Tell The River I shall Pray Again,' by Vinita Agrawal)

At first I hesitated to undertake the mammoth task of writing about the larger-than- life character that was my father. I was plagued by many questions and doubts. Would I be able to do justice to his spirit? Would I be able to capture the quintessential Nissim Ezekiel, not as a poet, but as the father that he was to me? Would I be able to pay enough tribute to this man with few needs, an 'unworldly man', a man we had to share with so many others, a man the family sometimes found difficult to understand? Would

I be able to convey our pain and suffering along with the joys and blessings of having him as a father? He possessed all the lovable yet bewildering eccentricities of a man single-mindedly devoted to his calling… a man with a great sense of humor, an entertainer, a sage, a guru, a storyteller and a conjurer of words that made magic on the page…a man who loved The Beatles, Simon and Garfunkel and classical music, as much as he loved Walt Whitman, Ezra Pound, T.S. Eliot and e e cummings.

Despite my doubts about undertaking this marathon task, on the 100th Anniversary of his birth, I have undertaken to write a personal memoir and put together a collection of poems dedicated to him. Included in the volume is a section in which I have invited poets, friends, family, and students who knew him, to share their memories, interviews and anecdotes about him.

> *'Writing a book is hard, you are giving yourself away. 'But if you love, you want to give yourself. You write as you are impelled to write, about man and his problems. You write about yourself because in the long run all man's problems are the same, his human needs of sustenance and love.'*
> Dorothy Day

In his professional capacity, Nissim Ezekiel was poet, playwright, professor, editor, critic. To my mother he would be her husband, and to my siblings and I, he would be the man whose blood ran in our veins. Preserving his legacy as a poet and a father is something very near and dear to my heart, even more important than my own writing. The rich literary inheritance my father left me, comes with a great deal of pride but with an equal amount of responsibility, if not more. This collection is not a set of critical essays but a personal tribute to my father, in honor of the Centennial year of his birth. It is purely a labor of love, with words straight from the heart. This is a personal memoir based on memories of my childhood and youth, and grapples with the terrible loss of his death, of trying to let go of the pain and suffering of being unable to be there by his side, in his last years. My poem 'Loss,' describes my grief at losing him.

Loss
(Dedicated to my father
who sadly passed away from Alzheimer's in 2004)

*My father could not talk to me
Before he died
Could not reach me in a distant land
Twinned in spirit, separated by geography,
I heard he remembered me
Said he could never forget me
Memory without a memory
Not able to remember
Not able to forget
Trapped in a maze of loss.
Two losses
The greater loss is mine*

Thankfully,

*He could not remember
What he had lost.*

In 1964 my father was invited to be a visiting professor at the University of Leeds. My mother had accompanied him. They also did a bit of sightseeing and he wrote regularly to us about his experiences. I wish I had preserved all the postcards. This one was shared by my sister. On a lighter note, this memoir is not written in the style of writing like the Bronte sisters, but it is as true and faithful to the memories and the indelible bond I shared with my father.

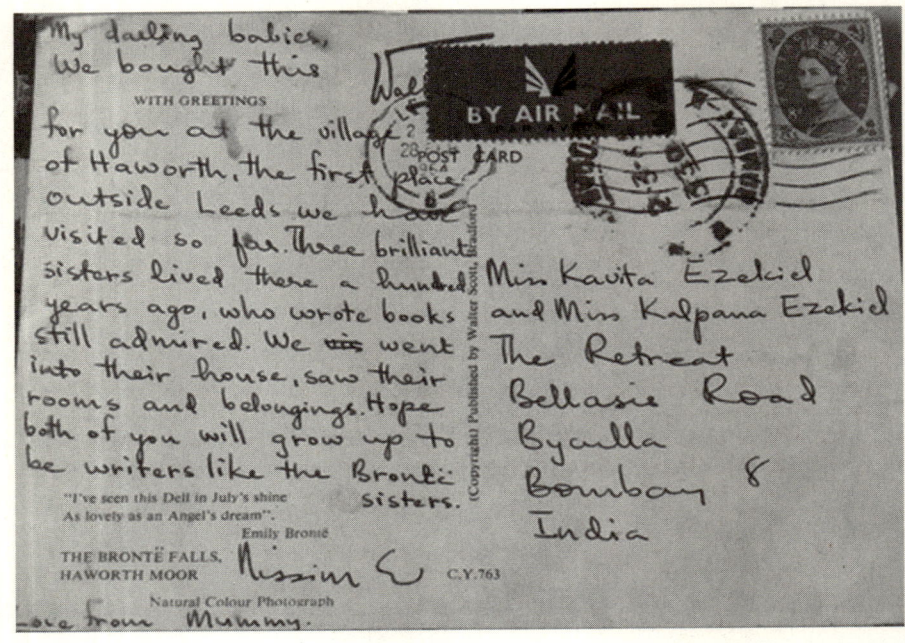

My darling babies,
We bought this
WITH GREETINGS
for you at the village
of Haworth, the first place
outside Leeds we have
visited so far. Three brilliant
sisters lived there a hundred
years ago, who wrote books
still admired. We went
into their house, saw their
rooms and belongings. Hope
both of you will grow up to
be writers like the Brontë
sisters.

"I've seen this Dell in July's shine
As lovely as an Angel's dream".
          Emily Brontë

THE BRONTË FALLS,
HAWORTH MOOR
          Natural Colour Photograph
          C.Y.763

Nissim E

Love from Mummy.

Miss Kavita Ezekiel
and Miss Kalpana Ezekiel
The Retreat
Bellasie Road
Byculla
Bombay 8
India

BY AIR MAIL
POST CARD

*'A memoir forces me to stop and remember carefully. It is
an exercise in truth. In a memoir I look at myself, my life
and the people I love the most in the mirror of the blank
screen. In a memoir, feelings are more important than
facts, and to write honestly, I have to confront my demons.'*
Isabel Allende

A Different Beginning

One Saturday morning a young girl, about ten years of age,
carrying a small suitcase with all her worldly goods in it,
walked down the lane from her home, and hailed a taxi. Her
mother had said she must go and live with her father after he
had decided to leave us. "At least one child should be with him",
she had repeated that sentence quite often. The little girl never
thought for a moment that mother's words would actually come
true. She had heard mother say them, seemingly under her
breath, yet loudly enough for her to hear. This time it was to be

different. Mother added that the girl was very close to her father and was always "daddy's little girl". When she had an injection, she cried for her daddy. Mummy reminded her that she had borne the labor pains, not her daddy! It was daddy she turned to for everything. Each time the girl said or did something, she heard the words "just like daddy".

Mother often joked about the umbilical cord being attached to her father instead of to her.

Anyway, the young girl did as she was told about going to live with daddy, because she had no choice in the matter. Nobody said goodbye to her. She kept looking back at the house to see if someone would be standing at the top of the stone steps of the ground floor flat, and waving. But there was no one there. She got into the taxi and gave the driver her grandmother's address, where her father was now living. The girl wanted to cry, but the taxi driver was watching her in the rear-view mirror. Perhaps he thought the child was running away. She was afraid, very afraid. She held back the tears and the fear. She wanted to get out of the yellow and black taxi and run back into the house. But the taxi had already begun to move. She clutched the suitcase tightly. School uniforms and tennis shoes were a must.

Ironically, daddy's favorite song was 'She's Leaving Home', by the Beatles from the album 'Sergeant Pepper's Lonely Hearts Club Band.' We shared a common love of The Beatles. Daddy said I should memorize my Shakespeare in the same way that I knew all the Beatles lyrics by heart! He knew this particular song by the Beatles by heart though. That was just a Shakespearean aside, simply alluding to the fact that I was leaving home. Unlike in the song, I did not have to leave a note 'clutching a handkerchief.'

If there was the slightest hint of foreshadowing in my narration, the reader would have guessed that the young girl in question was me. Since I was the eldest, I was the chosen one. The die was cast. I was to grow up without a mother, although she was alive. I loved my father dearly but missed my mother terribly. The bond I already shared with my father deepened. It did not dawn on any of us three children, how profound an event this separation between my mother and father would be, and the long-lasting effect it would have on us. My siblings would grow up without a father, and my mother without her husband. She became a single mother with three children. For us children, it was a terrifying situation, full of fear, uncertainty and doubt. The world had begun to take on the color of a permanent darkness. We were young children after all; we simply wanted to play and dance and sing. Isn't that what all children want?

(*Picture of Diana Ezekiel, my paternal grandmother*)

How I left Home for Grandma's
Kavita Ezekiel Mendonca

Leaving home was a simple act
Mother told me I must go
Now
Not tomorrow.

With few possessions it was easy
Pack the small suitcase
Hail a passing cab
Can't remember
If she gave me money
Must have
Or how could I go
Now
Not tomorrow.

At ten or eleven
Ponytails and curly headed
No hugs or kisses from
Mother or siblings
Just left as I was told
Then
Not the next day.

Grandma was waiting
'Everything will be alright' she said
With the Indian shake of the head
Small bed and small cupboard
Especially for you
You are small so no problem
You can have your own key now
Eat something Aunt has made
Just for you as welcome
Unpack tomorrow
Not now, later.

The first night was hard
Crying pillow-soaking tears
Missing mother, the garden and the sea
Here the pigeons in the high ceiling

Promised eternal companionship
I was afraid to make friends with them
What if I could go back home
Not now
But maybe tomorrow?
Then I would miss the pigeons.

Father came home at eleven
The creaking middle step
On the old wooden staircase
Announced his coming
He rang the bell loud and long
Called my name affectionately 'Kavitam'
He did the Indian headshake too
Just like grandma
'Everything will be alright'
Sleep now, it's late
Sleep now, wake up early
'Seize the night'
Now, not tomorrow.

The taps gushed water
At five in the morning
All life came alive
The servant woke me
Take a bath now
Or from water stored
In brass pots
May not be sufficient
For your long hair
Bathe now, the water may not come
Tomorrow.

I grew from girl to woman
The pigeons stayed my friends
The neighbors too
Cousins aunts and uncles
Came and went
I remained
Waiting to go home
Someday, perhaps tomorrow.

They took me to their homes
Weekends and holidays
Sent me home
Back to the pigeons
For school or work
Must go Now and
Not tomorrow.

I would still like to go home
But tall buildings and faster traffic
Have changed the garden and the people
Only the sea can't go anywhere
So I can take a walk
Now
Or whenever I want.

Now I am not home
Or at Grandma's
And I want to go
To both homes
Not tomorrow but now.

No pigeons here
No high rafters for their roosting
Water flows

When you turn on the faucet
A fancy word for tap
Not then but now
And will be so tomorrow.

This is the very first time I am sharing my story. Stopping at various stages, becoming quite emotional, as I am sure anyone can imagine, is part of writing a personal memoir. It has been hard to erase the pain of leaving my mother, though I have succeeded in rising above it for my own sanity and peace of mind. Daddy would have wanted me to do that.

In the words of Yung Pueblo *'If the pain was deep, you will have to let it go many times.'*

It is easy to tell someone to let go of the past, but much harder to do in reality, as those who have suffered any kind of trauma know well. While watching a TV program about the pandemic vaccination, I heard a woman in a rural area of my city describing her childhood trauma in a particular context. For the first time I was able to put a name to my experience. It was called childhood trauma. Before that I simply spoke of it as my past. Another phrase I came across from a writer in the context of her childhood, though I cannot remember exactly who the writer was, was 'insufficient childhood.' I thought it a particularly apt description of my own childhood, growing up without my mother and my siblings.

In every kind of writing I do, whether it be poetry or non-fiction, I find it easy to be honest, to tell the truth without glossing over the details, except when it comes to safeguarding the privacy of family members. Therefore, my memoir is based on the life-changing events that I unwittingly became a part of, while in its telling, I must respect the privacy of my siblings and my late parents. To their credit, they never spoke of their personal lives publicly. My mother never gave interviews to magazines or newspapers. She maintained she had three children growing up, and that it was important to protect them from any kind of publicity, since my father was a public figure. She was a simple person who did not crave wealth or fame, or any desire to live overseas. Her one wish was to have my father devote more time to his family. My father was interviewed often about his literary achievements but he too did not speak about his personal life in public. He was very reserved where that was concerned. We were never splashed across the pages of the popular magazines of the time. I remember being quite shocked and offended at some of the family scandals of other public figures that made headlines. Thankfully, at least, both parents spared us such intrusion into our young lives. Every family has its traumas and, for us, my father being a public figure, meant our personal space and his, must remain out of bounds. Or, it descends to the level of speculation and gossip. The truth is only known to those intimately involved. My father made no mention to anyone, of how or why I was sent to live with him as a young girl. Those who knew it were relatives, close friends and neighbors.

The 'Authorized Biography' – Poetic Injustice

'At the best of times, Nissim Ezekiel
was absent-minded and forgetful...
One wonders, then, would he now approve
of a biography that paints, in gory detail, the
decline of a fine poet and professor into a pathetic
near-invalid, stricken with Alzheimer's, who cannot
recognize faces, who's committed to a hospital'
Quote taken from P. Lal's
Bombay's Mr. Verse deserves better – India Today

Unfortunately, when my father was losing his memory, some who were in his circle of students and friends, took it upon themselves to expose in print his personal life to the world, through gossip and in graphic detail. The family was never in agreement with a biography being written, and were not consulted before the information was made public. The manuscript was never shown to us for our approval. The personal information was a complete invasion of our privacy as a family. It has hurt us to the core. Had my father had been in full command of all his senses and seen the manuscript, he would not have agreed to the publication of the biography. The long interview by an aunt was completely out of order. It was sad to read some of the biased and unwarranted personal criticism of my mother, without any compassion shown for the suffering she had to endure. Also, there were some incorrect facts in that interview. I have a good relationship with the children of this aunt, my first cousins, so I will refrain from further comment on the subject. She did live at my grandmother's house for a couple of months with her three children, and her treatment of me was less than a happy experience. My father took me into his room and reassured me that she was there only for a short while. His endless optimism when stressful events occurred was admirable, but confusing to me at that tender age. Having no mother to 'bat' for me made my aunt's treatment of me, hurtful. All my other aunts were like mothers to me. Another of my aunts declined to give an interview to the biographer. She has my deepest respect for her sense of discretion, and for protecting our privacy. My father would have respected such a response.

Of course a poet must have his critics, and my father took all the criticism levelled at him in his stride, though that is a different matter. However, when I read in the biography of their criticism of his craft of poetry or his 'lack of knowledge and awareness' in certain 'modern' areas, I often wonder why so many of his fiercest critics spent so much time at the P.E.N. office hanging around him, while he so generously spent all his time helping them hone their craft and publish their poems! My father never monetized his craft. He even edited manuscripts unrelated to poetry. When my mother asked him when he would do his own work, his reply was 'I will make time for it.' He functioned on very little sleep. When he was invited to speak at various events, asked what his charges were, he said, 'Give whatever you want.' If he felt the amount was too much, he protested!

One poet gave five reasons why he disliked Nissim Ezekiel. It seemed my father's claim about being lonely was simply a ploy to get attention. It was the same poet whose father had taken him to see my father for mentorship on poetry! I would be more than offended if someone made light of my 'loneliness' as simply a way to get attention without a real understanding of what I was going through. Though it might be a well-worn cliché, you really do have to walk in someone else's shoes in order to fully experience their inner turmoil, and not rush to judgment.

Apparently, one reason cited by a poet for disliking Nissim Ezekiel was that Ezekiel supported the ban on Salman Rushdie. The truth is very different. My husband, Alan was having lunch with my father at a South Indian Restaurant near my grandmother's house. They got talking, and Alan asked him about the issue. My father responded by saying that it was not that he was against freedom of expression, in fact quite the contrary, he was all for it. His fear was that the common man would misunderstand the reference, not able to see it fully in its context, (never having read the book), take up arms, become insulted and offended, and that for my father "was not worth the hair on the head of a single child." If religious leaders declared that what Salman Rushdie wrote in his novel 'Satanic Verses', was offensive and insulting to their prophet, then that would be taken as the truth. The fatwa was indeed issued against Mr. Rushdie, and he had to go into hiding. The world has now witnessed the horrifying attack on him, causing him to suffer life-altering damage to his body and mind.

The so-called 'authorized biography' was disrespectful to my father and undermined the kind of contribution he made to the literary world, both nationally and internationally. When he agreed to sit down, Saturday after Saturday, and answer the questions by the biographer, he assumed his literary journey was being documented. My father was a trusting man and took the biographer at his word. He did not even mention to the biographer that I had lived with him at my grandmother's house from the age of ten.

I was teaching at the international school in the North of India when I received a set of fifteen questions from the biographer. The first question was 'Who was your father's favorite daughter.' I remember telling my husband that this sounded like some kind of amateur writer. Of course, I did not answer the questions, though I had initially said I would respond. My father loved all three of us equally. That aside, for the same reasons as my mother and father, I guarded the personal lives of my parents fiercely. I too had a husband and two young children, not to mention my students and the faculty of the school where I was teaching. It is for the same reason that I did not respond to the biography publicly. So many of the facts mentioned are also incorrect and misleading. For instance, I was mentioned as the younger daughter, when in fact I am the eldest.

I will always owe my parents a debt of gratitude for their consideration and discretion in keeping our family life separate from the public life my father was invariably a part of.

The fact that the biographer has described the biography as 'authorized' is something that cannot be accepted. Only the parts where my father responds to the questions about his professional work and professional relationships are authorized. Also, in the biography, aside from several incorrect facts, there were several comments allegedly made by a Mr. X! Now that my father has passed on, perhaps Mr. X might like to reveal himself, so that the mystery can be solved, and my father's soul may rest in peace. Sounded more like the biographer was reveling in a gossip session rather than writing a biography of a poet who was a foundational figure in Modern Indian Poetry in English. Mr. X's comments, and other intimate details have cheapened the biography. The biographer seemed to enjoy documenting how many people my father 'fell out with.' In truth, my father was a pleasant and genial man who got along well with everyone with his 'live and let live' attitude. He was an outspoken critic though, and when he felt strongly about the value of a literary work, he did not hesitate to express his thoughts. I did not think that being outspoken is equated with 'falling out.' Contrary to the biographer's assertions, my father's high standards in relation to novels and essays will be evident to anyone who has read even a sample of his writing.

I quote from P. Lal's review in support of my strong objections to the biography. He was, to my father, a good friend, fellow poet, and renowned publisher. Sadly, he was never contacted for an interview for the book.

*https://www.indiatoday.in/magazine/society-the-arts/
books/story/20000515-book-review-nissim-ezekiel-by-r.-raj-
rao-777553-2000-05-15*

Issue date: May 15, 2000
Updated December 28, 2012

Bombay's Mr. Verse Deserves Better
Documentation carelessly slips into paparazzo voyeurism in this 402-page exhaustive biography of one of the father figures of modern Indian poetry in English.

"All biographies are selective. What makes a good biography is, among other things, the quality of the selection. Since this is the "authorized" biography of Nissim Ezekiel, one asks: who authorized it? Presumably, Nissim himself. "When I began my research, Nissim was still able to recall most of his early life for me. By the time I was finished, his memory had almost completely let him down."

"Nissim's family was uncooperative from the start.".... His daughter Kavita refused to reply to Raj Rao's questionnaire."

When I read in Raj Rao that Nissim and I "fell out", I was astonished. No way. We were, and still are, friends. True, he encouraged the ironical, experimental and oh-so-clever Bombay Group of poets, and I prefer the Tagorean romantic-idealistic, more desi song-birds – but surely there's room for both in the mansion of the Muses.

Omissions notwithstanding, this biography is a wondrous ragbag trove of useful material, but with an unnecessary excess of gossip, rumor and trivia.

Philanthropist Father

My father did not have the time or the know how to do any domestic chores. It would simply not enter his mind. He operated in an altogether different dimension. Everything domestic fell to my mother. She singlehandedly held the fort, did the cooking and other household chores, the banking and investments, helping us with our homework, understanding French grammar, particularly the verbs, English, Hindi and Marathi stories and poems, and of course the Math. She was an excellent Mathematics teacher, herself. All three of us would sit on the stone steps with her in the middle and she would ask us to note down the specific questions we had about each subject. She said she "did not have time to teach a whole chapter of anything." She attended my school Sports Days, standing up in the stands and calling out loudly "Come on, Kavita!" as I took part in the relays and other races. She knew I loved athletics. She was present at Parent/Teacher interviews and Prize-giving ceremonies. My father attended only one interview. My English teacher was particularly thrilled to meet him and was complimentary about my performance in class. He did however attend a performance of one of my choir concerts when I sang with the Cantata choir.

In the biography there was much criticism of my mother based on the perceptions of some individuals. Contrary to the opinions of those individuals, my mother was not money-minded or 'difficult'. Firstly, since my father did not understand much about money, and secondly being a magnanimous soul, giving his own money to needy people that came begging around our home, wherever he encountered them, and writing cheques for what he considered worthy causes, it became my mother's responsibility to ensure that there was sufficient money for household expenses and our needs as children. While she scrimped and saved, he gave his money to publishing poetry, starting poetry journals, and to social work. That was his passion. I was walking behind him once and watched him giving money to a complete stranger. When one thinks of a philanthropist, one imagines a millionaire with plenty of money to donate to causes of their choice. On a college lecturer's salary and with a family to provide for, my father's actions proved a real challenge for my mother. Most times he did not even tell her where or how he spent his money. My father donated his Sahitya Akademi Award prize money to a charitable organization. He told me once that if he did not have a family, he would give all his money to social work.

Finding Forgiveness and Healing

I forgave my mother many years later. I had become a mother myself, and was able to appreciate, from a fresh perspective, how she had done the best she could in a difficult situation. When I went to see her in the nursing home in 2005, she said the only thing she felt guilty about was sending me away to live with my father. She said she was sorry, and I began to weep. Meeting her after eight long years was overwhelming.

> *Mother apologises for sending me away*
> *It's the only thing she says she regrets*
> *in her life*
> *I visit her in the old-age home*
> *Her face is expressionless*
> *I weep.*
> *'Why are you crying?' she says, 'I did say I'm sorry.'*
> *But I was more than sorry*
> *What she didn't know*
> *I was sorry she didn't have a better life.*
> (Concluding lines from my poem 'At Seventeen.')

Of course, the act of separation from my mother and my siblings created a deep loneliness which I sometimes struggle with to this day. Fortunately, though we all shared a common 'traumatic experience,' each of us have made the choice to move on with our lives. We have a close relationship with each other, choosing to remember the happier family times we shared. We laugh about the eccentricities of our parents and acknowledge that humour is the only way to deal with our pain. It is my brother who has my father's sense of humor, and our phone calls to each other are made so much more enjoyable because of this trait.

On Sunday mornings I regularly listen to Oprah on the programme Super Soul Sunday. One Sunday she was interviewing the journalist David Brooks about his book 'The Second Mountain.' He said something while describing a lonely time in his life which struck a deep chord in me. He said, and I quote:

"Loneliness is a pain in the stomach." I have felt that pain and often that pain returns though I strive hard to push it to the deepest depths of my soul."

I did not think there was much to forgive my father for, at the time, as I lived with him and I adored him. I was acutely aware though, of the time he gave to others, the precious time he could have spent with the family. My mother felt strongly about his lack of attention to my writing and expressed it to him openly and often. If I ever even hinted that my parents 'ruined' my life, as I sometimes felt, my father would caution "each person is responsible for their own soul," and "happiness is a choice." There was no playing the blame game where he was concerned. And as for the childhood rant "I hate all of you", he emphasized that hate was too strong a word, and I recall literally being forbidden to use it. Instead he said I should substitute the word 'dislike' for 'hate'. When difficult memories surface, I simply want to turn back time. Knowing the impossibility of doing so, I turn to prayer. Every family has its tragedies, none are spared. Many have suffered greater tragedies than mine, though at the time it was not easy to look at my suffering in that way. Now, I often find comfort in the words of my father's poem 'Acceptance':

> *I am alone*
> *And you are alone.*
> *So why can't we be alone together?*

In a broader sense, my father and I were alone together.

Looking after Father

So it came to be that I became the natural caregiver of my father. It was something I was happy to do and took pride in. He simply expressed his appreciation with a smile and that characteristic twinkle of his eyes. That was sufficient gratitude for me, though none was needed. I simply wanted to make sure that he was comfortable. I changed the linen on his bed, dusted and organized the dresser, washed his hairbrush and other accessories that were on the dresser, scrubbed the floor and walls of the small washroom in his room with 'Vim', and filled and refilled the brass water container with fresh water each day. I also washed some of his clothes which we could not give to the servant to wash. She swept and swabbed his room but he felt it quite unnecessary that she should do that task daily. He felt that it was exploitation of the help. Like my grandmother, he had a special empathy for the poor and disadvantaged.

The task I enjoyed most was dusting and organizing the books stored in a small glass cupboard in his room. Copies of his books of poetry were housed there along with the set of twenty-four books which had been awarded to him for standing first in English Literature at the University of Bombay MA examinations. The inscription, with the seal of the University of Bombay read – '*The Ramchandra Lagu Prize for 1947 awarded to Mr. Nissim Ezekiel of Wilson College Bombay for having passed the MA examination with the highest marks in English.'* The signature at the bottom was from the University Registrar. The only surviving book is the collected works of Blake, which remains in my possession. I wish I knew the fate of the other twenty-three books and the volumes of poetry authored by him. Still, I have always lived by the dictum, 'Count not what is lost but what is gained.' It would be a miracle if they were returned to me and my siblings. They are part of our treasured inheritance.

 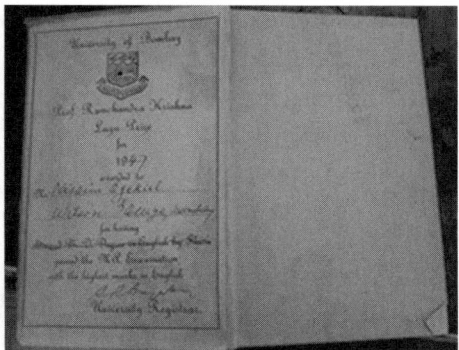

The Beginning of the End

On the night of August 15, India's Independence Day, my father said he had some work to do at the PEN office, although it was a holiday. He did not return home for dinner and there was no sign of him as the night wore on. My mother, along with her two little girls watched through the window, late into the night to see if we could catch sight of him walking through the garden leading to our home. My sister fell asleep, and I continued to watch with my mother till morning broke. My brother who was just a baby then, slept soundly through the whole ordeal. My mother taking the earliest bus she could, went to inform my grandmother of our missing father. He was there at her house, having breakfast, and told my mother he had decided not to come home and that he was going to leave the family.

In one night we became a broken family. If you come from a broken family it is as if you spend a lifetime collecting broken bits of glass and try to piece them together, in an attempt to form some kind of meaningful pattern. At my friends' and neighbors' homes where I was extended hospitality, the adults whispered (loudly enough for me to hear) in all kinds of languages, "she comes from a broken home." At times, I was embarrassed by their pity, though they had me over for meals, stepping in to become a family of sorts. This is the beauty of India, but despite their sincere efforts, I still experienced a great loneliness inside. I stood for hours on end at the window in my grandmother's house, consumed by this loneliness, separated from my mother and my siblings.

> *I stand at the window*
> *in a house full of people*
> *My loneliness, undiagnosed.*
> *The window is green,*
> *that's just the color of the paint*
> *My world has a different color.*
> *They don't put you in a hospital*
> *for loneliness, you must find*
> *your own cure.*
> *The love of a mother perhaps?*
> (Lines from my poem 'At Seventeen')

That loneliness, described by David Brooks as 'a pain in the stomach,' dominated my young life. I even contemplated 'another option to living.' ('At Seventeen'). Father had left us all to start a new life for himself. For some time, he had been telling us it was time to have his freedom, not from us, but to do his work without interruption. I do not know if any of us took him seriously. It seemed it was something he had repeated like a chorus in his own mind. Anyway, to this day I do not think he had really intended to leave us. He loved us too much. He simply wanted to do his life's work without the shackles of domesticity. The things expected of him as a family man were impossible for him to do. I believe he did want to come back to the family, but somehow that dream was never realized. Mummy told me she would let me cry, and that I would get over it in time. She told me she was too hurt to take him back. Though I understood her feelings, I found it difficult to accept and kept hanging on to hope.

Like all other things in my father's life, I still believed it was just another one of his experiments. How did I come to believe this? He would be back every evening before going to his new home, to sit in the living room, silently, with an expression that is difficult to describe. He would only ask for a glass of cold water, which I would bring to him from the fridge.

The moment he called my name, as he entered the house, I would throw my arms around him and weep loudly. "Come back daddy", I would say. "Alright, alright, I'll think about it, no need to cry" he would say calmly. *Calm* was his usual manner, something I recognize as a characteristic of the Ezekiel family. For a moment, I would believe him, but come eight o'clock, he would pick up his briefcase and prepare to leave. I would walk with him to the end of the lane and beg him not to go. "Alright, alright", he would say reassuringly, and leave. Sometimes, I would accompany him to the bus stop. Each time Bus No. 63, pulled away, I experienced a sinking feeling, wanting to flag the bus down and bring him back to our home, but the bus kept moving, taking daddy away from me. I would walk back home dejectedly, in the darkness. We ate dinner without him. The empty place at the table was a painful reminder of his absence. The fun and laughter had disappeared.

For a few days my father would go to a small guest house but that was not financially viable. My grandmother felt that by living at her house, he would have more connection with us. He would live in that house for the rest of his life until he needed full-time care and was moved to a nursing home. Tragically, his body and mind would be ravaged by Alzheimer's.

I would live with him till I got married. That cemented our bond further.

He chose the independence day of my country to pursue his independence. I am certain that was not a deliberately chosen date. That the two events coincided was simply ironic. Each time that date comes around, it brings with it a whole host of heartbreaking memories.

I celebrate this momentous occasion with the country of my birth, but deep down inside I still cannot resist the temptation to fervently wish for a reversal of events for my family. I had only one prayer and one wish growing up. Somehow my parents would find themselves back to each other and we would go back to our Family Sundays, as described in my poem 'Family Sunday.'

> *We call it a Family Reunion:*
> *my father makes his Sunday joke*
> *about Eliot's play,*
> *my mother laughs alone,*
> *They both agree*
> *that this is the way*
> *to spend a happy Sunday evening.*
> *We children*
> *are supposed to be content*
> *and not want a change.*

I wanted to go back to a time when we would sit on the stone steps together, eat homemade ice-cream and the pink blancmange in the blue ice-cream cups, daddy teaching me to ride a bicycle, and having long dinner times in the Spanish tradition of sobremesa (literally meaning, 'over the table') with daddy entertaining us by telling his wonderful stories of all his travels. Time stood still then. Mummy's voice trying to get us to clear the dinner table as she needed to sleep, still rings in my ears. She had to wake up at 4:30 a.m. to fry the onions for the curry! There were lunches to pack for school, and household chores to be done before helping the kids with their homework and studying for tests and exams. As a parent now myself, I empathize with her concerns. Back then, being young, it was all fun and games, leaving Mummy to worry about all the problems of life. Mummy said Daddy had only to worry about his teaching and his poetry! "Your daddy may be a poet", she often said, "but someone has to cook the meals, run the house, and look after the children."

'The Retreat' and Breach Candy: Two Different Worlds

My grandmother's home, 'The Retreat', built in the days of the British in 1894, was a collection of seven two-storey bungalows – very different from my home by the sea with its large garden outside the ground floor rented flat. The inside of grandmother's house was large and airy with the roof open to the sky. The stars were beautiful here too, but the openness of the roof created some sort of fear in me.

The monsoon roof open to the sky,
Frightening the child with hidden monsters,
Real or imagined...
('The Poetry of Homes', Kavita Ezekiel Mendonca)

There was a lemon tree outside one of the rooms and a spiral staircase at the back of the house, where cats could often be seen lounging lazily on the iron steps. At night the cats fought fiercely and sounded like crying children. Fear seemed to be my constant companion. Clearly, I needed my mother, but she seemed so far away in another home, though it was just a bus ride away.

Outside the large, wrought-iron gate of the Retreat, there was a small shop selling everything from sweet cigarettes, bull's eye sweets that every Indian child loves (my grandfather always kept a jar full of these) and real cigarettes, among other provisions. When I arrived at the shop, the shopkeeper knew exactly what I wanted and addressed me endearingly as 'baby'. Next to the shop was a hole-in-the-wall bakery, where my grandmother went to buy the fresh hot bread at precisely seven each morning. She dressed in a freshly ironed saree with her hair neatly tied in a bun at the nape of her neck. Beside the bakery was a small laundry and a restaurant, with wonderful aromas of biryani and kebabs tempting the senses. Such a lineup of bustling activity, all on one sidewalk, and of course the horse stables! When there was a fire, the horses would run wildly down the street, neighing, and whinnying frantically. A fleeing horse, or two, would enter the compound of 'The Retreat', and I watched the majestic creature from the window. Compared to Breach Candy, it was a noisy neighborhood with an abundance of people, schools, vendors, animals, traffic and religious places of worship. It had an old-world charm about it, which I now yearn for. It was another world altogether.

On the other side of the large gate was a '*pyaliwalla*', selling Indian street food consisting of a spicy chickpeas dish with sweet and spicy chutneys and garnished with cilantro. There was always a large crowd gathered around him. The customers were mostly schoolgirls from the school in the adjacent compound and from the other school across the street, among other customers. The girls' school in the next compound operated in shifts and a row of school buses were parked on our narrow street. The excited chatter of the girls seemed to fill the sky!

I felt like the ground was torn away from under my feet, though I was at my grandmother's house. I lived in a constant state of 'missing something.' I missed going for walks with family and friends, to the beach to eat *Bhel puri*, and to the Hanging Gardens at the top of Malabar Hill, where we could look out at the spectacular view of the Queen's Necklace and eat samosas with green chutney at the Café Naaz. I missed the family outings to the Kwality restaurant where the favorite dish was Rogan Josh with soft, fluffy piping hot Naans. I missed the smell of the sea, the sound of the waves crashing on the rocks, the white spray as it blew into the air. I missed sitting on so many late nights out in the garden outside the house, dragging the chairs from the dining table, an irreplaceable experience. I missed sitting on the stone steps with my siblings and sometimes a cousin or two. I missed my friends who congregated there to play, chat and share stories, every evening after school. I missed Violet aunty, my neighbor in the next building who made the best garlic bread in the world, and gentle Ariel uncle and their sweet children Jennifer and Christopher. There was always a piñata in the shape of a plane for Christopher's birthday. I missed Minnie aunty who made the best *Dhansak*, a Parsi curry, served with rice and meat and cutlets. Minnie aunty was especially partial to me!

Most of all I missed Daddy in countless ways… daddy standing in the middle of the living room singing melodiously *'Trees', 'Sounds of Silence'* and *'Home on the Range', 'It's a long Way to Tipperary,'* and *'Till the Lights of London shine again,'* Daddy taking me for orange and vanilla stick ice cream at the store, or to buy a bottle of *Vino Royale* "to celebrate life." He did not need an excuse to celebrate. For a treat, he bought chocolate ice cream, which I savored as it was chocolate covered vanilla ice cream. I missed daddy reciting *'The Night Before Christmas,'* and *'Bells, Bells, Bells'* by Edgar Allan Poe, Daddy putting his arms around mummy, singing *'Give me Five Minutes More in Your Arms,'* and mummy protesting vociferously and squirming out of his embrace.

While living at The Retreat, my father was busy with his teaching and his writing and various other assignments. He would leave early morning and arrive late at night. At exactly eleven pm, the middle step of the old wooden stair of our building would creak, the bell would ring twice and his voice affectionately calling my name '*Kavitam*' would have me rushing to the door to greet him and welcome him home. He had walked from Bombay Central Station, a good ten- or fifteen-minute walk to the house. If he had had a long day, he never complained. He remained cool, calm collected, taking everything in his stride. I rarely saw him angry, but when he lost his temper, he pronounced my name by biting his lower lip, *Kavitam!*, not *Kavita*. Then you stood at a distance, and timidly asked what crime you had committed. You trembled to think what the consequences could be, but usually it was some kind of gentle admonition with a touch of philosophical advice.

Cousin Nissim comes to stay

One of the best times at my grandmother's home was when my cousin Nissim, a few years older than I, came from America to do his bachelor's degree at St. Xavier's college in Bombay. The largest room in the house was divided by a partition with a small door; his room was on one side, and mine on the other. We had a close relationship, our common love of music bringing us many shared moments of fun and enjoyment. Nissim was a young man of many talents. He was dedicated to his studies and played rhythm guitar in a band called '*The Combustibles*.' I went everywhere with him. He included me in all his activities. When a new 45rpm vinyl record was released, Nissim would take me with him on Bus No.65 to Rhythm House where he would buy the record. Sometimes we walked to Clare Road to buy a record from the music shop run by Mr. A.B. Moses. Nissim had cousins on his mother's side, and I would accompany him to their home. The best part of Nissim's stay was that he owned a transistor radio with a black leather case. On Saturday nights, he would lend me the radio and, while he studied, I put the radio under my pillow and listened to the songs on the music program, '*Saturday Night Date*,' lying on my stomach. Nissim had beautiful handwriting, like in his notes on National Income which he lent me to study for my Economics exam. He was, and is to this day, a meticulously organized person. I wonder if Nissim realized how much his presence in my life at that time brought the much-needed glimmer of light and hope in some of my darkest and loneliest hours. The most important thing we shared was that we were both brought directly from the hospital to our grandmother's home as newborns. If not for the love and care my aunt Hannah lavished on me, I would never have survived. "Next year in the Promised Land," she would say. Her move to Israel was my great loss, and I missed her presence in my life dearly.

Here is my poem dedicated to her followed by a picture of my aunt Hannah with my cousin Nissim and myself.

Light of the Sabbath

Sacred Fridays of the Sabbath lamps,
An aunt's faithful hands squeeze grapes
She allows me to squeeze just a few.
Purple juice-stained hands in purple glass,
Steady purple flame rising to Him who listens,
Meaning of *The Shema revealed.
Hebrew, English and Marathi prayers flood the room.
God is a linguist, understands all languages,
He doesn't need a translator.

The Sabbath done, she rubbed my hair with coconut oil,
Sleeping with news-papered pillow till morning,
Washing out the oil till hair lights shone
By her same hands of faith that lit the lamps,
Cooked red mutton curry, coconut rice
On her room-corner kerosene stove,
Saturday evening, the sun gone to bed.

Those hands that move mountains
Stirred the curry, fluffed the rice.
'Faith may move mountains.'

The Lord said, 'Let there be light,'
The Sabbath light, the light of a hundred and fifty Psalms,
Her faithful reading on Saturdays.

Each Friday evening we squeezed
The purple Grapes of Faith,
And each Saturday she read
All one hundred and fifty Psalms,
Head covered with the saree scarf
Her Godly body swaying slightly
Lips moving in whispering prayerful devotion.

* The Shema – Jewish prayer:
Hear O' Israel, the Lord is our God, the Lord is One.

(Published in the Fall 2020 issue of the Harbinger Asylum,
ed. Dustin Pickering; as well as, later, in my chapbook
'Light of The Sabbath')

Decades later, I would receive an exciting email from my
cousin, which I was delighted to read, about the connection

between Shimon Peres and my father. That is narrated fully in an interview with Urna Bose (included in the Interviews section). I also shared that story in a special Zoom presentation in 2020 on my father, at the invitation of the Indian Jewish Heritage Center and the Cochin Heritage Center in Tel Aviv, Israel, in which Nissim also participated. And it was so lovely of Nissim to host a well-attended poetry reading in his home for my father when he once visited Washington DC. Nissim and I continue to remain in close contact with one another.

"It Takes a Village"

At the Retreat I was raised by the proverbial village. Extended family, cousins, friends, and neighbors filled my lonely hours with the fun and love a child craves. I would be remiss if I did not make special mention of my beautiful and charming aunt Asha Bhende, my Lily aatyah (nee Ezekiel, *aatyah* is father's sister in Marathi) and my quiet, unassuming uncle Atmaram Bhende, a veteran actor on the Marathi stage. Lily aatyah was my father's younger sister, and I was a constant presence at their house in Chembur. It was like a second home to me. Very often I would spend my weekends there. My uncle would call me from his office in Worli and ask me to be ready to be picked up and driven to their home. The beautiful bungalow was opposite the bungalow of the famous actor, Raj Kapoor, who was incidentally a classmate of my father in school. It was a long drive, and my uncle was a very quiet man. I chatted away while he listened and smiled from time to time. Once at their home, I was their third child. The food was wonderful, the vibrant and exciting company of my two cousins Purnima, and her brother, the legendary singer Nandu Bhende, not much older than me, was a treat. My Sarah aatyah (my father's eldest sister) had a laugh that tinkled like bells. She came in laughing through the door and was always good company.

When I first arrived, I developed severe pain in all my joints. It was diagnosed as rheumatoid arthritis. I remember my grandmother telling me it was all just due to stress, and I would get better soon. It was my aunt Sarah, a doctor, who brought some sort of 'cold to the touch' liquid in a large brown bottle. She soaked a couple of homemade cloth strips for bandages and placed them on my knees and elbows. I was asked to rest on the large bed in my father's room. Gradually, I improved with their love and care.

Her handsome, charming husband Srini kaka (*kaka* is 'uncle') was universally adored by all of us. He was a Navy man with impeccable manners. When he said 'How are you, beta?', you felt you were part of his family, along with my cousins Vijay, Geeta and Radhika. My father spent many happy visits to their home and their hospitality to him, and to us, when I stayed with them with my husband and son, was full of warmth. I could have belonged as a daughter to any of these families. My uncle Joe (my father's eldest brother) was a tall man with a commanding voice and fun to be around. My uncle Hanaan was quiet (the quietest) but exuded intelligence. He was a well-known economist, and was for some years, the editor of the Economic Times. His wife, my aunt Ivy, was lively and enthusiastic about everything in life, whether it was cooking or singing or knitting sweaters. She kept a beautiful home, and my cousins Nissim, David and Rebecca were great friends to me. Rebecca and I share a very close bond to this day. We both live in Canada, and she has been a wonderful supporter of my writing journey. We exchange phone calls and messages regularly. We reminisce about our college days, about the music we listened to, about the discos we danced in night after night, and about the boys we liked.

My grandmother, whom we called '*Aai*,' which means mother in Marathi, was the matriarch of the family. She was the glue that held us all together. Calm and soft spoken with grey-green eyes, she was mother hen, shielding all fourteen of us cousins under her wings. She loved each one of us unconditionally without favoring one over the other. My *papa* (my paternal grandfather) sported a moustache which never ceased to amuse me, since I watched him once brushing his hair and moustache with his hairbrush! He wrote a book about the Bene-Israel Jews of India and insisted that we chew our food thoroughly. To demonstrate he would make those movements with his jaw like a cow chewing the cud!

My paternal grandparents, Moses and Diana Ezekiel

(My grandmother with her grandchildren…
one of my cousins was away in America)

To the families of my neighbors who adopted me, I say 'Thank you.' My dear friends Zulekha and Aban were my lifelines. I was often at Zulekha's house eating meals with them from a common 'thaal,' which is a large plate. We sat on a mat with her entire family, and broke bread together. Zulekha's mother also made the best mutton samosas. Aban's mother never forgot my love of mutton *Dhansak*. She sent Aban to call me whenever she cooked this favorite dish! My deepest gratitude to my school friend Sunita, who would pick me up on Sundays with her dad and her brother in their small red car at precisely ten in the morning and bring me to their house to spend the day. They would drop me back to 'The Retreat' at six in the evening. Then, I spent hours standing at the window feeling terribly lonely, wondering why I was separated from my family. To my many college friends, and friends at the University, who have made life worth living, I say 'Thank you!' To the many friends in St. Xavier's College, especially Lyla, Abby and Piroja, Brenda and Joy, for their friendship, I owe so much for all the fun they brought into my life. The boys in the group, Thomas, Rustom and Ivan, were chivalrous and caring.

Impossible to forget the large extended maternal family, without whose love I would have starved... Ivy aunty who often rescued me from my strict mother, immortalized in the poem 'China Grass Halwa', Mozel aunty who made the best 'Bombils.' In English, 'Bombils' are called Bombay Duck. They are not ducks but a kind of glutinous fish with whiskers. My aunt would fry them crisp, and diligently remove all the whiskers, whenever she knew I was coming over for a meal. Then there was my Sheila Mami (Mami is mother's brother's wife) who nurtured my love of the Hindi language and was the kindest, most loving, forbearing, and patient person you could ever meet. Her home was about a fifteen- or twenty-minute walk from my grandmother's home. My mother's eldest sister Sarah, whom we called Doctor Aunty, strict and firm but generous to a fault, was always there when I needed her. Ruby Aunty of my poem 'Alibaug', who 'put ten chillies in the curry when I visited/her usual was twenty'... and whose home was my second childhood home. I had so many second homes! I know now, as I knew then, how blessed I was.

With great affection, I recall my kind, generous and loving uncles on my mother's side. Large-hearted Shalom Uncle who loved cricket and was awarded best batsman at Lloyds bank, who took me often to the restaurant for exotic meals, soft spoken and gentle Joe Uncle, and fun and lively Aaron Uncle who teased me mercilessly all in the name of good fun, Judah uncle who lived in Alibaug:

> My uncle owned a grain mill
> He was a jovial man with a rich laugh
> The grain poured out of the ancient machines
> Like his patient and unselfish love for us.
> (Lines from my poem 'Alibaug')

My cousins Isaac and Lilu, are also celebrated in my poem 'Alibaug', where I spent so many wonderful holidays as a child, Samson Uncle, whom you could always count on for the wisest counsel on marriage, parenting and everything in between, who taught me the meaning of love, and an appreciation of the National Geographic, and to whose home I could go in joy or in distress. And I can never forget Shalom uncle's words to my mother, after my father left the house: "Daisy, bring the three children and come and live with me. You do not need to be alone." He had the smallest of flats, but we were welcome, and what was most important to me was that I felt wanted. The feeling of being wanted was something I needed and held dear.

To have two sets of grandparents in my life was a double blessing. I believed from my grandmother's actions that, for some reason, she was partial to me and had an extra special place for me in her heart. I describe my maternal grandmother, whom we called Ma, in my poem 'The Ballad of Little Ma':

If measured correctly
Little Ma was four feet, eleven inches tall,
Or even smaller,
That's how she got her name.
Her real name was Leah, grandfather called her Lily.

There's more to Little Ma.
With kindness in her actions
She spoke less and placed her hand
on your shoulder, to tell you,
that she loved you.

My maternal grandfather, Isaac Jacob, always wore a white kurta-pajama and sat on his large bed by the window, singing a song about the gentle breeze that flowed into the room. I wrote a poem in Marathi, in which I recalled the song, and how the memories of him singing return whenever a gentle breeze flows through the windows of my home.

A Few Daddy Stories as told by Mother

The first few years growing up seemed to be happy and carefree, an almost ideal childhood, with an abundance of love from both parents. Mother told some stories about how daddy 'spoilt' me. She constantly lamented the fact that he was an indulgent father.

When I was about a year old my father had to go to New York for work. The suitcase was packed and locked. As the time to leave for the airport approached, my father could not find the keys. The hunt was on, with no luck. Finally, he left for the airport. After he had gone, my mother discovered that I had taken the keys and hidden them in the 'stomach' (that part of the doll where the sound box was located) of the Walkie Talkie doll. I missed my father terribly and developed a bad case of blisters on my head. The doctor's verdict was not a medical diagnosis but a psychological one. He said I was pining for my father and the blisters would only go away when he returned. At my maternal grandmother's home, my aunt Ivy would wash my hair with a gentle hand as my mother expressed impatience with the situation. She is the very same aunt who left for Israel, the loving aunt whom I have immortalized in my poem 'China Grass Halwa':

Who will save me from mother
When she became angry and impatient with me?

One of the daddy stories I love best was the one my mother often narrated to me even when I had grown children of my own. I was three years old when my father would walk me to the nursery school, a play school, a few minutes down the road from our rented home in Bombay. The school was above a small store called Premsons which later expanded to a bigger one, selling all kinds of expensive luxury items. My father would come to pick me up after school was done. He enjoyed doing that and looked forward to it each day. Well, I wanted to hop off the ledges that divided the shops from the sidewalk (foot path, as we called it those days), so we would be quite late coming home. My mother, becoming worried about the delay, would repeatedly ask why we took so long returning home when the school was just a five-minute walk from home. My father patiently explained to her about the 'child' wanting to jump off the ledges and she would say "And you let her, you are such an indulgent father, you just don't know how to say no." His response was the same as always "she's just a child, let her have the experience."

At nine years old, I was suddenly taken up with the idea of boarding school. Mother was completely against it as she felt it would be like running two 'establishments.' She always used the word 'establishment' as if we were the Queen's household! Daddy's mantra was "let her have the experience." So, the application was made, and admission granted. The school I was attending in Bombay agreed to save a spot for me for one year. So off I went with my father agreeing to take me to Panchgani, a small hill resort town, an eight-hour bumpy ride from Bombay, on a State Transport bus. On the way, the bus had an accident and was leaning heavily against a tree. I got out through the emergency window. My father got out when the bus was finally made to stand upright, with all four wheels on the road.

Daddy had to return to Bombay the next day as his glasses needed repair and there was no optical store in the little mountain town. Meanwhile we held it together with rubber bands. Mother thought the accident was a bad omen. "See!", she said. "I told you not to let her go!"

Boarding school was not what I had imagined it to be. I cried bitterly for my mother and wanted to return home immediately. The other little girls tried in vain to comfort me. I was inconsolable.

The matron of my first dormitory was a kindly woman named Ms. Reinhardt. She had two large Siamese cats, whose eyes glowed frighteningly in the dark when we returned from night study hall. My father wrote his daily postcard to me. He tried his best to provide words of comfort and encouragement. The postcards were placed at the foot of my bed when I came to the dorm for a short break after lunch, before going back for the rest of the school day. The other girls were amazed. A postcard a day! They were lucky if they got one a month! Sometimes he wrote me longer messages on those green inland letters. I wish I had kept the postcards and the inland letters. So many precious memories lost in transit. The dorm room, the bed with the postcards in daddy's unmistakable handwriting, have never left my memory.

When he was invited to be a visiting professor at the University of Leeds in 1964, my mother accompanied him. She told me that one night at dinner, he got a lump in his throat and could not eat the marrow from the bone of the piece of meat because it reminded him of his children left behind, so far away. Of all things, they had packed the marrow spoon in their luggage, quite certain they would not find one available in England! Back home, it was always my father's job to use the marrow spoon and give some to my sister and I, often holding the spoon with the marrow directly to our mouths when there was a meat bone with the rich juicy marrow in it. He missed his two little girls dearly. We were being cared for by my grandmother in Bombay. His postcards to us speak of his love. They are addressed to 'My darlings Kavita and Kalpana.'

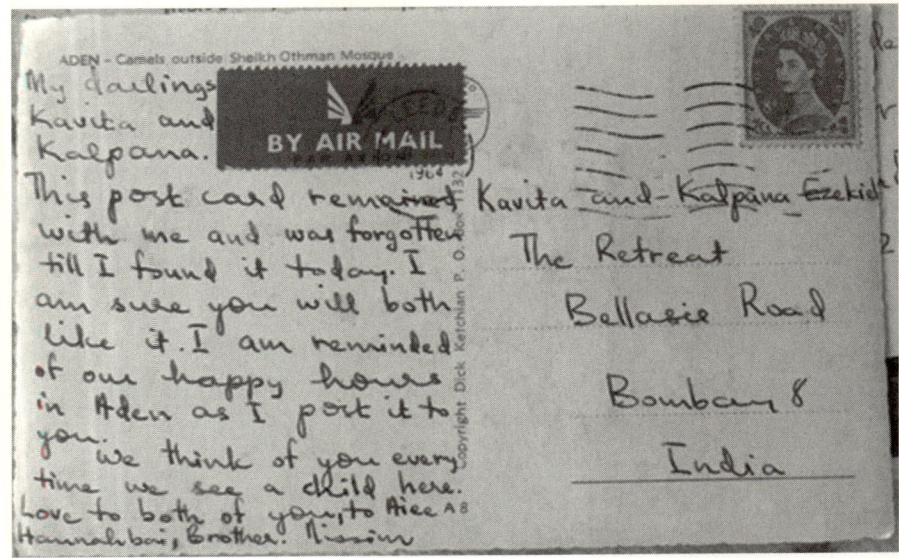

By far the funniest story my mother narrated was the one about our visit to the home of the Principal of her school. One of my aunts, my mother's older sister, had also accompanied us. I was very young then. For some reason, I had developed a great taste for clean and well-designed washrooms. So, the first thing I asked the Principal was if I could inspect her bathroom. Even if she thought it a strange request, she still complied. I emerged from the washroom and declared that I did not like it at all. Later, the Principal asked me how my father was doing. I replied that he was 'too clever by half.' This is an English proverb which means too clever for your own good. My mother told me she did not flinch when I uttered those words. As the conversation was all in Marathi, it sounds more colorful in that vernacular. The English translation somehow just does not do justice to it! I guess the Principal was good humored and took it all in her stride.

Mother had an idiom for everything,
Some she recited in English, others in Marathi
If you failed a math test, it was

'Don't cry over spilt milk,'
She said my daddy was 'too clever by half'* (sounded better in Marathi)
If he rationalized matters by 'clever' intellectual arguments,
Remember he was a poet!
One day she took me to see the Principal of her old school
Who asked how my daddy was
My reply, 'my daddy is too clever by half.'
Mother did not flinch when the Principal asked
Where I had learned that expression.
(From my poem 'Mother.')

In December each year, along with my husband and children, I travelled down to Bombay from the mountains, for a two-month vacation. The International School where we were working in the North of India, was closed for the winter. One year, we arrived completely exhausted from the long journey, with our two toddlers. After lunch we fell into a deep sleep, the two little ones between us. We continued sleeping till the early hours of the evening. Daddy had just returned home from work, when he heard the cries of our little one. He came into the room and picked her up in his arms. We slept on, completely oblivious to the crying or the scene that was unfolding in the living room. Mummy told us that daddy rocked her in his arm for six hours! She kept asking him to wake us up and attend to the child. She reminded him that we were the parents and that it was our responsibility to take care of the child's needs. Later, when we asked him why he did not set her down, he replied that he had attempted to do so, but each time he tried, she began to cry. When my husband heard what had happened his comment was "That's just like daddy." I agreed... it was typical of daddy – kind, compassionate, always putting the needs of others before himself. I told him that the baby was wet and simply needed to be changed. He replied gently, "Well, how was I supposed to know that?" He had never changed the diapers of his own children but had sung to them and rocked them in his arms. Perhaps even recited some poetry to them! Takes me back to a time when I recall how sometimes, when my mother was busy in the kitchen, he sat us on his lap and did his writing.

The photograph above is of my sister Kalpana sitting on my father's lap, at the desk where he did his writing.

The Memories Continue

I last met both my parents in 1997 when I came to Bombay for my winter vacation, from the international school in the foothills of the Himalayan Mountains where I had been teaching English for the previous 16 years. This was when I first gave the news of moving to Canada, to my parents, separately though. My mother's reaction was in these words, "Let me tell you something for the first time now, when you were born, your father rejoiced, he thought he had written his best poem," I recalled the evening I was attending a poetry reading of his, with my family, when he was asked which his favorite poem was. He promptly replied with the usual twinkle in his eye, "My eldest daughter, Kavita."

Then after a long sigh my mother continued, "your father won't be at all happy that you are going so far away from him". I was already beginning to feel the loss of separation from my father, and the excitement of the new adventure became greatly diminished. When I talked to my father, he said, "Don't go, you will be lost, this country is your home, and you should stay here." "You will regret it," he continued. I guess when one is young, one thinks one is invincible. There was so much valuable advice my father gave me which I did not heed. How I wish I had taken this piece of advice to heart. I am now lost in so many ways, too many to name, but my greatest loss still remains the void created by his passing.

'You don't really know how attached you are until you move away, until you've experienced what it means to be dislodged, a cork floating on the ocean of another place.'
(Michelle Obama in her memoir 'Becoming')

My father loved all his children equally and never made any differences between us. When I wanted to follow a boyfriend abroad to pursue a degree, my father denied my request. He told me in no uncertain terms that he had three children, and if he sent one, then he would have to do the same for the other two. He could not afford that. So, I remained in India and completed my education there. I had to be content with writing long letters to my friend.

A first-born child always holds that extra special place in a parent's affection. However, due to complicated family circumstances, I would live with him from the age of ten, soon after he moved to my grandmother's home, and we became a nuclear family of our own. In an interview with Urna Bose, I explained how the bond between my father and I was further cemented by the common circumstances we found ourselves in. Organizing his wardrobes, washing the clothes that needed washing separately from the others, dusting the hundreds of books, many of which were signed by poets from around the world, and going shopping with him to help him buy the colorful Khadi kurtas he wore, were enjoyable, as daddy was wonderful company. He would say, "Now, now, don't overdo things; a little dust never harmed anybody." That was Daddy... always philosophical and impractical in worldly matters (with so much dust in Bombay, one had to clean daily), but well-meaning at all times.

Through so many indications, also recounted in that interview, my father spoke of his wonderful love for me as when he narrated how, while in New York, a photograph of mine he had carried with him, spoke to him telling him I was the extension of his soul on earth. The very fact that he carried the photograph with him to New York on one of his trips meant so much to me.

I recall the time when I told him that I was going to get married, way back in 1980. He said, "Don't you think you can stay with us a little while longer?" I couldn't believe I was hearing right. I was twenty-six years old and in those days it would be considered quite late for an Indian girl to remain unmarried. At every stage, he seemed to be coming up with a reason I should stay close to him. Then he proceeded to add that I should do my MPhil and PhD and that if I got married one thing would lead to another. I asked him what he meant. "You know children and all that sort of thing, with little chance of coming back to it." He had, in mind, Osmania University in Hyderabad, and mentioned that "Isaac Sequeira was a good man and would look in on me from time to time so I would have nothing to worry about." I had met Professor Sequeira in Bangalore some years earlier. He was a wonderful individual, kind, gentle, magnanimous and with a hearty laugh, but nothing could change my decision… I was determined to marry.

In 1992, when I was studying at Oxford Brookes University, my father had received an invitation from the Arts Council of Britain. He told us that he really did not want to travel but would accept the invitation so he could visit us in Oxford and spend two days enjoying our company. We hosted a dinner and poetry reading for our tutors, and he delighted us by reading his poems and telling stories and jokes too! One of our tutors asked him if he had ever heard of Graham Greene. My father was quite taken aback and said, "Who hasn't heard of Graham Greene?" The tutor did not know anything about my father's background, and said he was surprised that an Indian poet was so well acquainted with the works of Graham Greene. And he asked my father if he wrote his poems in English or in *Indian*! He meant Hindi, of course.

When my father visited the international school in Mussoorie where I was teaching, he interacted closely with some of the students in my Advanced Placement English class, as well as reading his poems at the High school Assembly. Even after an exhausting journey, long after the family had all gone to bed, he stayed up till two in the morning writing a poem for two of the students who showed him the way to our home at the top of the hill. He titled the poem 'Lost and Found in Mussoorie.' He gave a handwritten copy to each girl. One of the girls preserved the poem and kindly sent it to me, which I have included in the poems section. It is a poem in my father's unmistakable handwriting. The girls were thrilled when he read out the poem dedicated to them, in the school assembly.

There's actually quite a story behind his visit. He had been to Delhi to attend a Board meeting of a certain organization and mentioned to one of his delegates that his daughter lived in Mussoorie. They told him it was just a short bus ride away and that he must make the visit. After an eight-hour ride, he arrived at the bus depot and then took a cab to the school. The cab driver was completely unaware of the direction to his destination. When he arrived at Cozy Corner, a small food stall at the bottom of the hill, selling omelets and Maggie noodles popular with the students, he met two young girls. They brought him all the way up the hill to our home. When the doorbell rang, we were thrilled to see Daddy with the two students. He later confessed that he would go to any length to be with me and my family. Much later, the girls told me they were supposed to be in the dorm but had snuck out and broken the curfew! Call it fate, luck, or chance they were there to help daddy find his way to us! Daddy wrote about them in a poem:

The moon did not show the way/But two stars did...

Leaving Daddy Behind

Soon after I arrived in Canada, Daddy was diagnosed with Alzheimer's. My brother gave me the devastating news. I couldn't imagine Daddy's brilliant mind being ravaged in that way. My brother told me that he would not be giving me any updates on his condition, and I should remember him as he was. Once, he gave me a brief inkling about what was happening to him, visualizing daddy like that was heartbreaking and unbearable.

Visiting his grave with my brother, a year after he died was almost a surreal experience. As I stood there at the Jewish cemetery in Mumbai, on a grey day with a slight drizzle falling, I felt he was still alive.

I stood beside my father's grave
At the old Jewish cemetery across the racecourse
There was his poem about a shooting star
Engraved on it with a Star of David,
I thought I heard him recite the poem
I wept, careful not to erase the lines
His voice mellifluous and poignant
He made me fall in love with poetry.
(From 'My Father taught me Love.'
Kavita Ezekiel Mendonca)

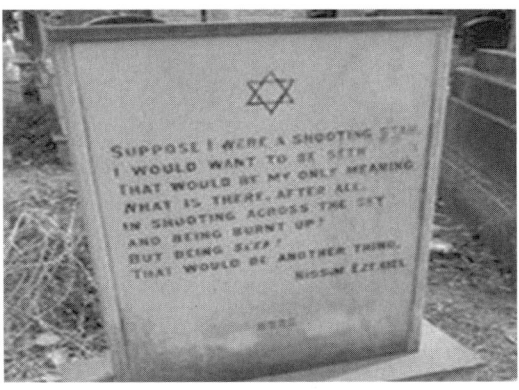

Lessons from the Bumblebee and Shakespeare

Along with books with *'forgotten cheques becoming bookmarks of a different kind,'* (words from my poem, 'How Daddy Wrote His Poetry'), a turtle shaped coin box for *'loose change'* (Daddy's words), and lined paper with lines of poems on them, there was a large black and white version of a poster with a picture of a bumblebee on it. These were permanent fixtures on his desk. The words on the poster read, *'According to the law of aerodynamics, the bumblebee cannot fly. The bumblebee does not know this, so it goes ahead and flies anyway.'* He lived his life inspired and driven by this philosophy. It was this poster that inspired my love of bumblebees, as well as the message to persevere despite limitations. His other special mantras were *'Peace at all costs,'* and *'Happiness is a choice.'* He often quoted Thoreau's words, *'I went to the woods because I wished to live deliberately.'* The emphasis was on living deliberately. I learnt to live my life with a purpose, not to drift aimlessly and take things as they happened to me. My purpose, apart from a passion for teaching and writing, included my love for my family and my deep faith in God, inherited from my mother. Her mantra was *'God is great,'* and I find myself living a much more fulfilling and meaningful life anchored by the faith in her words. She imparted her values and practical wisdom to me, through proverbs and sayings. There were the common ones *'Don't cry over spilt milk,'* and *'Waste not, want not,'* but the most important lesson I learned was reflected in Shakespeare's words which she never quoted, but demonstrated in her own life:

'Neither a lender nor a borrower be,' and *'Give few thy ear and fewer still thy voice.'*

I learned from her actions, not to meddle in other people's business, and to keep my own counsel.

My father taught me the value of hard work, to be sincere, genuine, authentic and honest, quoting Shakespeare's words from his play Hamlet:

This above all to thine own self be true
And it must follow as the night the day
Thou canst not then be false to any man.

He taught kindness to others, and never to look over your shoulder at what everyone else was doing but to do the best one can do personally. To illustrate this, he narrated the story of the marathon runner who was winning the race when he decided to look over his shoulder to see who was behind him. In a split second, the other runner overtook him and won the race. My father's teaching was one of non-competition with others, instead to compete with oneself to do better and better. His advice has stood me in good stead, especially in these days of Social Media.

I waited for Daddy for so many reasons, but I also waited for Daddy for the amazing love he brought in what might seem to others something so small and insignificant – a packet of peanuts. Daddy never put his arms around me, hugged or kissed me, or made any outward demonstration of love but expressed his deep love and caring in numerous ways.

Peanuts that do not come wrapped in a cone-shaped newspaper package, which Daddy brought home regularly for me from the peanut seller, can never taste as good. Good things surely come in small packages.

Happy 100th birthday, Daddy. I love you simply because you are my father. You are alive in every poem you wrote, and in every poem I write for you.

POETS, FRIENDS, STUDENTS AND FAMILY REMEMBER...

Portrait of Nissim Ezekiel, included here by courtesy of the well-known Indian painter, sculptor and muralist Jatin Das.

"We are all the pieces of what we remember.
We hold in ourselves the hopes and fears of those who love us.
As long as there is love and memory, there is no true loss."

Cassandra Clare, *City of Heavenly Fire*

Adil Jussawala

I don't remember exactly when I first met Nissim but it must have been in 1961, the year I left my studies at Oxford to be in India. We must have met at Mazda Mansion.

I think that's what the building was called – in the ground floor flat which he rented. I was staying with my parents then, further down the road, and I used to drop in often. I had written two plays and several poems during my four years in England and Nissim and I would talk about them and several other matters – cultural, political, social. Daisy and he were warmly welcoming.

I remember you and your sister Kalpana, young children at that time, being in the living room where Nissim and I sat and talked, Though both you and Kalpana were naturally restless, I remember both of you normally had books in your hands.

The reason I was drawn to Nissim was that I had first come across at least one of his poems in The Illustrated Weekly of India before I'd left for England in 1957. That poem was 'Midsummer Madness'. It was Nissim's response to domestic constrictions and since I too felt them as a teenager, it appealed to me. Our friendship developed.

As you know, Nissim helped get my first book, *Land's End*, published by P. Lal's Writers Workshop.

After I returned to Oxford in 1962, we corresponded. We met in England when he was at Leeds. I continued to read whatever he wrote with the greatest of interest – the exactness of thought in his prose, the concrete images of his verse, appealed to me. He was surprised when I criticized what I found to be a somewhat clichéd abstraction in one of his poems, in an article I wrote for The Journal of Commonwealth Literature. He was hurt, but we remained friends.

By the time I returned to India my political opinions had changed. My leftist assertions didn't suit Nissim and they sometimes got in the way of our friendship. But that friendship never broke. He was warm, understanding, and precise in his manner and speech until Alzheimer's struck him. I owe him a lot and continue to think of him as an indispensable friend and guide.

Alan Mendonca
Verses from a Poet's Life

Waiting for Daddy

Dusk falls quickly during November in the Himalayan foothills. In our home on the beautifully forested mountain on the outskirts of Mussoorie, we awaited an important visitor. He was scheduled to arrive at 5 PM at the boarding school gate where his daughter, Kavita, taught. I waited there till 6:30 PM but he did not turn up. I was now leaning against the fence outside our house, the flickering lights of Dehra Dun spread out before the dark mountains. The air had a nip to it and wonderful aromas of Himalayan oak fires and curry wafted from the few houses below. I went inside and switched on the TV – almost at once, the doorbell chimed. 'Hello, Kavitam' rang out – it was Dad, but with two young students in tow. They had been at the little restaurant at the base of the hill and Nissim had asked them for directions. They offered to bring him to our home. Good thing, too, because the dark mountain paths can be treacherous to the uninitiated.

The next day at Student Assembly, he was the guest speaker. We were surprised to hear that he had gone to bed at 2 AM, only after penning a poem in praise of the two young women who had been his guides the previous evening. '*The Moon did not show the way. Two stars did...*' he began. I do not remember the rest of the poem. What I do recall is Nissim's complete capture of the crowd of young hearts that day.

Satanic Verses

It was 1988 and I was in Mumbai for a course. I lived with Nissim in the sprawling, ramshackle flat at the 'Retreat' on Bellasis Road. The kitchen was not in operation, to put it mildly, and we would make our way together to the South Indian restaurant across the road for our supper. He mentioned casually to me that he was scheduled to give his views on the publication of Salman Rushdie's controversial novel, 'Satanic Verses'. I told him I was aware that there was a ban on its publication and that several prominent people had spoken out in favor of publishing it – freedom of speech and all that. He said he supported the ban. I was dumbfounded! I asked him why. He said that there was really nothing controversial in the novel, but the very fact that the offending parts had created such rage was enough to set off a bloodbath in the Indian context where the vast majority of people, stirred by the publicity, lived in squalor. Their fury would erupt in with murderous mobs rampaging through the *gullies* (lanes) and *mohallas* (neighbourhoods), their main victims being uncomprehending, innocent women and children. 'No amount of freedom of speech is worth the life of one child or mother', he said. I was certain he would be pilloried in the press. I do not recall if he was.

Water conservation and Criminal tendencies

As much as he was rational to a fault when discussing cerebral ideas, ideologies, and literature, a markedly different Nissim emerged when dealing with the mundane…

Each year, our little family would live with him in the Retreat during the winter. One of my first tasks was to ensure his room was 'spring' cleaned. Our children were granted territories – half the room each to tidy. As payment, they would each receive a few rupees they could use to buy goodies from the little paan shack outside the Retreat.

My next task was ensuring Nissim had a full, hot-water bath, complete with an infusion of Dettol. All year long, he would refuse to use running water and anything in excess of a bucket for bathing was flagrant waste. He'd remind us that most people in the street outside did not have access to running water. This was his way of empathizing with the needy and doing his bit for conservation. (He once chided a visiting journalist at the Taj Mahal Hotel for leaving lights on in her room, remonstrating with her with a "That's not the point" when she said "It's paid for"). All the same, his ineffectual ablutions made him smell mildly gamey. Once he had had his great bath, it was time to trim his toenails. He'd initially refuse maintaining that they looked perfectly fine. Eventually he would agree, and the ceremony would begin with a basin with warm water, a towel, and clippers. The trouble began as soon as I started clipping – it took work on account of their thickness – because Nissim would start swatting me with his newspaper and a speech: "people are put in jail for the sort of things you're doing. A doctor will need to be called for the injuries you are inflicting on me. Thousands of rupees will be wasted on treatment. What sort of criminal tendencies do you harbor? You don't seem to have any conscience at all". The speech was accompanied by throwing his hands in the air and the family loudly asking him to calm down.

A Precious *Meduvada*

One evening, upon arriving home, Nissim's trousers had a large oily stain on the outside of one of the side-pockets. Kavita asked him how he managed to get that stain. He said 'Oh, I almost forgot', and reached into his pocket and held out... a *meduvada*. He said, 'This was a delicious snack served today at the party – I thought you might enjoy it'. Without a word, Kavita took it, realizing that Daddy was only thinking of how much his daughter might enjoy it.

Cheese!

On his poetry-reading trips overseas, Nissim was given a list of precious 'foreign' items to bring back. His knowledge of these was non-existent but he always had a group of admirers who were more than willing to take him shopping! On one of his trips, Daisy had ordered him to bring back the best cheese in New York. What she meant was Kraft cheese. We welcomed Nissim back with his battered little suitcase and he set about opening it with all of us eagerly circling the suitcase. As soon as he did, an overpowering stench filled the room and he announced 'Daisum! The best cheese in New York! Just for you!' She looked at him with profound bitterness: Nissim, you hate me so much that you went out of your way to get me the smelliest, most rotten packet of cheese? In vain did he try to explain that an absolutely wonderful lady had gone out of her way to take him to a famous cheese store, and he had bought the most expensive cheese there – just for her! Oh, and the only other item was a large, heavy book – the collected works of Allen Ginsberg, who had been a friend from a long time ago. Just for Daisy! There were no other 'foreign' items.

New Year Gifts and more freedom of speech

His coming home from work during the Mumbai winter evenings was exciting, because of the gifts he would bring.

Nearing Christmas, one evening, he took me aside and reaching into his bag brought out the most delicious-looking box of chocolate-coated ginger and a bottle of Scotch. He said, 'This might be something you're interested in'. I asked him where he got these. He said that visiting poets and journalists often gave him little gifts and he would give them away to good friends who invited him for dinners, since he could not reciprocate in any other way. A cupboard was quickly cleared and I told him I would get him a collection of gifts for his friends, but that when he received precious items in bottles, they were to be stored on one shelf during the year. I would then introduce him to the joys of cocktails! We spent many evenings in the winters which followed quaffing the life-giving elixirs.

Funnily, he'd also receive expensive 'Calendars' from certain embassies with the map of Israel emphatically blacked out. He'd accept them with grace without any comment. During the first Iraq war, the Nagpada neighborhood was all agog with anti-American sentiment. He received a visit from a delegation of the local elders in the community who wanted to ask a special favor. They asked if he would be offended if they put up a banner across the road. He asked what it would say. They sheepishly replied, 'Death to Zionism'. He said 'Not at all. You're free to express yourself.'

Oblivious to Beauty

Nissim once asked me to join him for an evening's performance by a dance troupe from Israel at the NCPA. It was a wonderful performance, but after the show there were no taxis to be found and my little daughter adamantly refused to walk. In the middle of trying to cajole her to walk 'just a little', an absolutely stunning young woman came over and asked if she could give us a ride. Nissim politely agreed and got into the front seat with her. She said she could drop us to the Breach Candy flat where Daisy lived, but we insisted that Churchgate station was good enough.

She then said, 'Forgive me for asking, but are you Nissim Ezekiel, the poet'. When Nissim replied 'yes', she gushed with 'I love your poetry and I compose poems too!!' Nissim then asked her what she did for a living. She said, 'I was Miss India 19xx and I'm a model for a designer in Paris.' That explained the glamorous looks! When she dropped us off, Nissim asked me 'Alan, what is a Miss India? And what is a model?'. I stared at him, speechless.

The kindness of strangers
Kavita and I spent a sabbatical at Oxford in the early nineties. During that year, Nissim was invited to read his poems in England. He decided to first stop off at Oxford to spend a few days with us. I wrote him precise instructions on the bus service from Heathrow to Oxford. At the appointed time, I set out for the bus station on my bicycle with my daughter to receive him. After waiting for two hours, I decided to head back home, since Nissim had not turned up. There he was, in our living room, having a cup of tea with Kavita. When I asked him how he got to our place, he told me that a lady on the plane had offered to give him a ride to Oxford (she would be passing through) and drop him off at our home. She said she had met him on one of his poetry reading sessions on a boat ride on the Thames ten years earlier. 'Wow!!' we said admiringly. 'Who was she? What's her name'? Nissim replied 'I don't know; I can't recall meeting her.'

Talking at cross purposes.
Early in his career, Nissim was editor of the Imprint Magazine. A friend met him one day and asked, 'How many issues do you have?' Nissim replied that it was 20,000 the previous month and expected about the same for the next rollout. The friend was dumbfounded! 'Most people have two these days and may have three at the most! But you? You have so many?' He was talking about children.

Onset of Alzheimer's

By 1997, it was becoming clearer that Nissim was losing a great deal of his razor-sharp intellectual abilities. It was all there, but jumbled, confused and cross-wired. One morning, recovering from a cataract operation, he insisted on going to his office next to the Alliance Française at Churchgate. Kavita had a fiery argument with him, but to no avail. At around 2 PM, we received a call from an Irani restaurant owner who asked if we were in any way related to Nissim Ezekiel. I said 'yes'. He told me that he was concerned that an old man sitting at one of his tables was staring into space for a long while. When questioned about who he was, he could not answer. He had then taken the old man's wallet and found a paper inside with our name and telephone number (Kavita had quietly slipped it into Nissim's wallet weeks earlier) and decided to call. I took a cab and brought Nissim home. He sat silently through the ride. It has been many years since Nissim passed away after spending his last years at an old age home in Bandra. He was fortunate to have people who cared about him, like Elkana, Nissim's son, who ensured he lacked nothing during his stay in the Home.

We miss him.

Elkana Ezekiel
FOR ME HE WAS JUST 'DAD'

Growing up in Bombay, it took me a long time to realize the significance of the name, Nissim Ezekiel. My teachers frequently chided my inability to solve math problems by saying "Your father is such a great man, look at you". Somehow, it never bothered me and when I asked Dad about it, he merely laughed. My childhood memories of Dad were, like most kids, connected with play, toys, story-telling and outings. We lived at Breach Candy, on the ground floor of a Parsi owned estate called Mazda Mansion with our front door opening out into a lovely garden with jackfruit and custard apple trees, sunflowers, and money plants aplenty. Dad would patiently teach me cricket, though I fear his efforts were in vain. What I recall vividly was the morning when I hit the ball over the fence and onto the main road. In the late 60s and early 70s traffic was light, and Dad chased the ball till he had it in safe custody. I didn't preserve that ball, but instead I have this lovely memory.

The years rolled along, and I started becoming conscious of being in the company of a special person. Dad's poetry was winning acclaim, he received praise for his free-flowing style and every now and then his collections of poetry would be released, making him a household name. In our home, we learnt to recognize the signs when Dad was writing something new. He would grow silent and engage in several tell-tale activities. Some pranayama, loud enough to frighten away the neighborhood stray dogs, a few lines, a walk in the garden, a few lines, lying down with a crumpled hanky across his eyes, a few lines. Till finally it was done. Usually, the first person with whom he would share his new work was Mum. She had her own way of communicating with him and he valued her opinion enough to redo his work, if he agreed with her. This was one area where they were in harmony.

Dad was often invited to international poetry platforms, cultural festivals and as the guest of foreign governments to visit their top universities and exchange ideas with their intelligentsia. While all this is the stuff of legends, for me Dad's foreign trips meant only one thing – foreign shopping. In pre-liberalization India, foreign travel meant Levi's jeans, Adidas shoes, the latest music LPs and fine chocolate. I've lost track of the number of times Dad would return past midnight and the entire family would crowd around his suitcase from which magically appeared all the goodies we'd been dreaming of and more. He was a terrible shopper, never really understood what we wanted, but inevitably found some kind soul in those faraway lands who helped convert our unending shopping lists into reality.

When I reached the 10th standard in school, I found myself studying my Dad's poem, "The Night of the Scorpion", which was part of our ICSE board syllabus. My English teacher invited Dad to visit St. Mary's School where I was studying and address the students. So, I squirmed and beamed alternately as I sat in the audience while my beloved Dad was on stage sharing the sources of his inspiration, patiently explaining that poetry and writing were not work for him but a gift that he had been blessed with, one that he carried lightly.

The world knew him as Professor Nissim Ezekiel, India's pre-eminent Indian poet in the English language, Padma Shri, Sahitya Akademi Award winner, teacher par excellence, et. al.

I only knew him as Dad.

Fiona Fernandez

I am honoured that you would like to use my article as part of your father's centennial anniversary tributes. I feel extremely privileged. My late mother who was also a teacher, enjoyed your father's poetry each time we discussed it at home as it was part of my English literature syllabus in junior college. She would have been very happy.

This article first appeared in Mid-day dated December 17, 2021. COPYRIGHT/MID-DAY INFOMEDIA LTD.

Her father's daughter

INTRO: To commemorate his 97th birth anniversary, Nissim Ezekiel's daughter, Kavita, collaborated with poet Mustansir Dalvi to release the Marathi translations of two of his poems as well a third, an ode to her illustrious father

> *SUPPOSE I were a shooting star,*
> *I would want to be seen,*
> *that would be my only meaning,*
> *what is there, after all,*
> *in shooting across the sky*
> *and being burnt up?*
> *But being seen!*
> *That would be another thing.*
> – Nissim Ezekiel

On busy Dr E Moses Road is an oasis of calm. It is the Jewish Cemetery, the final resting place for Mumbai's Bene Israelis. Among those who are buried here is Nissim Ezekiel, the famous bard. His words (above) etched on his epitaph echo the journey and contribution of the community.

He may have belonged to one of India's tiniest minorities but Ezekiel, affectionately called 'The Poet of Bombay', played a key role in postcolonial literature in India, having impacted generations. To commemorate his 97th birth anniversary (December 16), his eldest daughter Kavita Ezekiel Mendonca collaborated with poet and academician Mustansir Dalvi to release Marathi translations of two of his famous poems, 'Poet, Lover, Birdwatcher' and 'Night of the Scorpion', as well as a third, 'Loss', that she penned about losing her father to Alzheimer's Disease in 2004.

Found in translation

"I read Professor Dalvi's translation of poems into Marathi on his Facebook page. Many were of poets my father admired, like William Carlos Williams and Rilke. I enjoyed his translations, and began communicating with him. Marathi is my first language along with English. It is the language of the Bene Israel community of Indian Jews. My husband and I also speak Marathi at home, although his first language is Konkani. My father had co-translated the poems of the well-known Marathi poet Indira Sant. Last week, I requested Professor Dalvi to translate my poem," shares Ezekiel's Canada-based daughter. "Professor Dalvi is an accomplished and widely published poet. I have been co-translating my father's poems into Spanish, and hope to translate them into French someday," she reveals.

For Dalvi, Nissim was a familiar, avuncular figure while he was at architecture school, walking around the same places as he did in South Bombay. "I saw Nissim before I read his poems in books at the British Library. He was easily recognizable because of his long flowing hair and metal-framed glasses. I was struck by his strong poetic lines, his observations, his use of language and how he got the everyday speech exactly right." Dalvi's favorites are 'Goodbye Party for Miss Pushpa T.S.' and 'The Patriot'.

He was well aware of the risks that come with this translation since he began translating from English to Marathi recently. "Most of my work is the other way round, translating Marathi poems into English. I attempted translating English poets, both Indian and international, to see how their poems sounded in Marathi, for my own pleasure. I am grateful to Kavita for urging me to translate Nissim's poetry, and her own ode to her father." Dalvi attempted these with some trepidation but feels he got the spirit of the poems. "Of course, they have to stand as Marathi poems on their own. The act of translation must be subsumed in the final product, never to stand out."

While working on these translations, two things struck Dalvi. "The atmospherics in the poem — night, rain, diabolic tail, very noir and the prayers that I tried to refashion with rhythmic incantations. It is poetry that sweeps in several directions, and I was aware of that while I tried to put the translation together."

Daddy's poetry

Kavita has fond memories of watching her father at work, "I watched with great interest and some amount of amusement, the process and technique my father employed in the writing of his poetry. I have described this in my poem, 'How Daddy Wrote His Poetry.' He usually took one puff of a Menthol Cool cigarette and left it to die out in the ashtray, placed a handkerchief over his eyes and lay down on the bed, then back to his desk after a few minutes as the lines came to him, writing them down on lined paper, then back to the bed again. It was a kind of a set rhythm," she reminisces. In comparison, Kavita writes at her desk, in the office space that she shares with her husband. "When I set out to write a poem, I am not conscious of my father's influence, but once I'm done writing and revising, I realize his strong influence. I have developed my own voice, but we share a few similar themes, such as a love of nature and ordinary things, as well as a more conversational and direct style of writing. Sometimes, even the tone of our poems is similar." She admits, however, that the depth and breadth in his writing will need many lifetimes to achieve. There is something about poetry that attracts children, both to read, and write it. And Kavita wrote poetry from an early age, though she did not think it had much to do with her father at that stage, except unconsciously. "He was quite excited though, that I had become interested in poetry. I had a long career in teaching in Indian schools and colleges, and in private schools overseas, and was deeply committed to the profession. I published my debut collection in 1989. Subsequently, there was a long hiatus, working full time, raising two children, and moving to another country. It was only after I retired that I resumed writing poetry. I enjoy writing, but it is hard work and my thoughts go back to my father with every poem I write. He juggled a full-time teaching career with his writing, mentoring other poets, and immersing himself in other interests like art and theatre."

Unlike the weight that offspring of successful people tend to carry, it was easy for Kavita. "My father never put any pressure on me to write. In fact, he said he felt people would think he was promoting his daughter. He was very conscious of that fact. I believe, from the messages I receive from individuals whom he mentored, that he was very proud of me. He even carried my first book of poetry (*Family Sunday and Other Poems*, 1989), with him to Israel, when he was invited there in 1995. I respected his wishes to not be involved in my writing, though it was a difficult decision, especially for my mother. He devoted all his time and energy to mentoring other younger poets. I am certain my writing career would have taken a much different turn if he had done the same for me."

Legacy matters

Kavita is keen to keep his legacy alive. She discusses his poetry with today's younger generations of poets, who might not be acquainted with it. "I also take every opportunity to introduce him to students of poetry overseas. My father was a foundational figure in the postcolonial literary history of India. Contemporary poetry cannot be studied in a vacuum." She is working on a personal memoir to commemorate the centennial anniversary of his birth. "It will be a challenge to record so many special memories of growing up with an interesting and 'larger than life character'. Every anniversary is a reminder of his wonderful achievements and how much fun it was to be in his company. He was a great storyteller. He also had a sweet tooth, though he ate everything in moderation, so we will celebrate with cake on this occasion!" she signs off.

Kavita, the poet

Kavita recalls a poetry reading session where Ezekiel was asked about his favorite poet. He replied, "My daughter, Kavita." That wasn't meant to exclude my siblings (he wrote poems about them too). He had named me symbolically, and perhaps, even prophetically! That might have had something to do with it. He had obviously put a lot of thought into my name.

Nissim and Bombay

Ezekiel had a deep commitment to the city of his birth; it featured in many of his poems. Kavita quotes from 'Island':

> *I cannot leave the island*
> *I was born here and belong.*

She also shares from 'Background Casually':

> *Others choose to give themselves*
> *In some remote and backward place*
> *My backward place is where I am.*

She had written poems to celebrate his love for the city and hers as well.

"As he grew older and needed to be cared for, I invited him to live with us in Mussoorie, where I was teaching English in an international school. He wanted to join us but did not wish to leave Bombay. Although many Jews left for Israel, he stayed back. He believed that if everyone left, 'who would do something for India?' He had wanted to do something for India from an early age. He was at home here, and specifically, in Bombay," she shares.

Gayatri Mazumdar
Responses to questions from Kavita Ezekiel Mendonca

When did you first meet my father, Nissim Ezekiel? Do you remember anything specific or special associated with that first encounter? Further encounters?
G: I believe it was in the late 1980s I first met Nissim Ezekiel. As an aspiring poet, I had heard of Poetry Circle and about their regular meetings held at Indian P.E.N.'s office in Theosophy Hall. Although there was nothing striking about the first encounter, I have an abiding image of a dimly lit room overflowing with books and papers with Nissim at its center working or reading. I was in my late twenties and in awe of him, but as others would concur, Nissim would always put us at ease almost at once. Several encounters followed and I would sometimes meet him at the Poetry Circle meetings which he would attend or over tea at a restaurant across the road where we hung around. He would blend in very easily with a group of poets in their twenty-somethings.

This was followed by several encounters with Nissim until around the mid-90s. Sometime in the early 90s, he needed someone to assist him to edit the *Indian P.E.N.* magazine, and I willingly agreed. This had a long-lasting impact on me; as someone who had just started to write, I found Nissim's guidance and support highly rewarding. I'm confident it's his belief in my passion and talent that shaped the way I evolved as a poet and publisher later on in life.

I met him again briefly in late 1990s when his memory had begun to fail.

What were your impressions of my father? How did these change, as you got to know him better?
G: I found Nissim to be a soft-spoken gentle person when I first met him. I rarely heard him raise his voice and, as editor of the

Indian P.E.N., he always backed my selection of contributors to the magazine and never questioned my decisions.

In retrospect, I recognize what a large-hearted magnanimous person he was! He made each one of us feel special and important, and treated us all equally. Apart from this, he also made himself available to every visitor who dropped by at Theosophy Hall. Nissim could be extremely involved yet detached, persuasive yet tender in a strange sort of way. His door was always open for whoever came in. He also had this delectable sense of humor.

Can you describe him in his professional work, such as writing, mentoring younger poets, art critic, working at the PEN?
G: What was remarkable about Nissim's approach to mentoring younger poets was that he believed that everyone had some potential. When he let the nascent poetry group (the Poetry Circle) meet at Theosophy Hall, he opened several avenues for them. He would go over their poems, publish their work; besides, it's here that younger poets were able to meet other poets/writers of great stature such as Aga Shahid Ali, Arvind Krishna Mehrotra, Pankaj Mishra, Imtiaz Dharker, Adil Jussawalla, Dom Moraes and several others.

Similarly, I had hardly ever known him to 'reject' any poem or piece of write-up submitted to the *Indian P.E.N.* This strengthened several poets' belief in their own ability. His very presence was reassuring, and whoever interacted with Nissim understood that they were a part of something extraordinary as well as enduring.

What is your favorite poem of my father's?
G: I love many of Nissim's poems, but my favorite has to be the one I published in *The Brown Critique*. This long unpublished poem, 'Whispers', which Nissim 'submitted' is the very first poem in *The Brown Critique*'s first issue way back in January 1995. It had a distinctive Zen-like tone to it and I consider each micro poem a meditative piece of writing.

Here are some lines from 'Whispers':

3.   *If you can't sleep,*
       remain awake peacefully.
       In the darkness, be darkness.

9.   *What I say to my soul*
       is not important.
       What my soul says to me
       lights up the universe.

20.   *I have faith in magic:*
       formulae, incantations, devices,
       mystic exercises
       and simple hard work.

Is there anything else you would like to add?
G: The poetry environment in India today has changed significantly. The learning and times spent at Nissim Ezekiel's P.E.N. office cannot ever be replicated – the camaraderie, the critiques, the sense of belonging to something larger than oneself. Nissim had a singular role in shaping our destiny as poets, publishers, critics and others. I'm truly grateful for having met Nissim so early on for I believe he is one of the reasons why poetry continues to be such an integral part of my life and work. Here's wishing Nissim's Centennial Year celebrations tremendous success. I would like to thank you, Kavita, and Vinita, for thinking of me to be a part of this phenomenal book.

Gieve Patel

At the age of 18 or 19, I had heard the name 'Nissim Ezekiel', and I had even read a few of his poems, but I did not personally know him, and I had never met him. It was my friend, the poet and actor Kersy Katrak, who said he would introduce me to Nissim, and that I should show some of my recent poems to him.

So I met Nissim, and I gave him a small packet of my poems. I approached him again after a month or so and asked him if he had seen the poems. He said yes, he had seen them. He did not seem to be impressed by them, and he said a couple of critical things. But he left the door open, he said he would like to see the next batch of poems that I might write.

I confess I felt discouraged, but I continued to read and to write. After almost a year I gave him a new batch of poems to read. This time I received a postcard – in those days we communicated with each other on these thin yellow ready-stamped postcards! He said he had read the new poems and had found them good. He invited me to have tea with him at his Warden Road home. I was not expecting this, and was no end pleased. Also intrigued to know what he might have to say.

The meeting and the tea have always remained memorable to me. He was hospitable, gentle, friendly, and he went over some of the poems with me and showed me their merit, pointing out to me how I had succeeded in achieving this or that effect. It was a lesson! I had been writing 'without thought'. He demonstrated that good poetry has a lot of thought behind it, and that a poet should be aware of his tools.

Nissim related to me right from the beginning with feelings of warmth and mutual regard. I had no feeling of uneasiness when I met him and spent time with him, although he was much older than me, and had a wonderful record of achievement. However, I did notice that with many other people he maintained an air of formality, almost a cool that seemed intended to keep them at a distance. I did not understand what made him hold himself so. Perhaps he did not wish to be overwhelmed by demands that people might make on him? I'm not sure.

All this changed as years wore on. He mellowed remarkably, and latterly ran almost an open house at the PEN office where he worked. He visibly enjoyed meeting people, and people came to meet him cheerfully. Around this time, even the tone of his public readings of his poetry changed. Whereas earlier you might say that the tone was a bit uptight, he now had started to read more directly to his audience. The audience sensed this, and responded in a like manner.

A writer will have a range of relationships with other writers in his environment. For Nissim, A. K. Ramanujan was a near contemporary. They shared a wonderful friendship, full of warmth and mutual regard.

In early years, Nissim was my mentor, not only for creative writing, but also in our general conversations about 'matters of the world'. Over the years this developed into a friendship. There was depth and concern in this friendship.

Nissim also reached out to a large number of other writers and journalists. Many of these were wonderfully talented people. But, more and more latterly, he was open to being approached by almost anyone who expressed a need for help. He was criticized for this by many observers who felt that he was abandoning the rigor that true critical appraisal calls for. My observation led me to believe that at this time in his life he was guided by a sense that no one who approaches one should be turned away empty handed.

Nissim's writings in the Times of India art column spanned a number of years. The art world looked forward to these weekly or bi-weekly reviews with anticipation. The reviews were characterized by an honest, candid approach. They were also insightful. He was, for instance, one of the first writers on art to recognize the importance of a painter like Bhupen Khakhar.

In fact, he predicted that this painter's work would develop astonishingly over the years. And this indeed did happen as he had said it would.

In the world of academics, Nissim's work at the University of Bombay is well-known. Since I was not directly involved with the university, I leave this section for others to comment upon.

I would like to end with an account of Nissim's interest in education per se. It is quite possible that this was derived from his closeness to his mother, who was a school principal, and who had a life-long association herself with school education. Nissim showed a great deal of interest in primary and high school education. I have a memory of him, after he returned from a trip to Goa, asking me to visit a school there. His eyes shone as he said: "This is grassroots education, the school has evolved from the very soil around."

Jeet Thayil
14 Attempts at a Tribute

Reprinted with Jeet Thayil's permission from *The Rediff Specials*,. Jeet Thayil is the author of *English* (Penguin, 2004)

1. Sometime in 1998, just before sitting on a plane that would get me out of Bombay, I went to see the poet Nissim Ezekiel. He was in his usual room at the PEN center, sitting alone at a dust-trap of a desk piled with periodicals, manuscripts, and books. I had called to ask if I could see him, but when I walked into the room it was clear he had not been expecting me.

It was an early indication of the Alzheimer's that would eventually claim him.

2. As we got up to leave the office a woman appeared, a clerk or typist. Will you be coming back, she asked. The poet Ezekiel frowned at her. Of course, he said, of course I'll be coming back. I'm going out for coffee. With that he stalked off, leaving the woman gazing after him with some consternation.

3. We walked across the street to a small restaurant that served coffee and South Indian snacks. Everybody knew him of course, but mixed with the familiarity was a kind of callousness. Uncle, what are you having? said the waiter who took our order. The poet Ezekiel appeared not to notice any unpleasantness; he smiled uncertainly, he was a small island of serenity. He wore a frayed blue and white shirt buttoned at the wrists, caked with dirt at cuff and collar. He was living somewhere in Marine Lines, in one room. He would commute by bus to the PEN office at Churchgate carrying a plastic bag full of possessions. I wondered how many of the people in that restaurant knew he was among the nation's most distinguished poets.

4. The poet Ezekiel was born in 1924 in Bombay. His parents were Bene-Israeli, secular Indian Jews. They spoke Marathi and English. His father was a professor of botany and zoology, later a college principal. His mother founded and ran a Marathi-medium school. In his early twenties he was a member of M N Roy's Radical Democratic Party. The year after Indian Independence he took off for England, on a one-way ticket given him by his friend, the legendary theater director, art collector and impresario Ebrahim Alkazi.

5. For three-and-a-half years in England, the poet Ezekiel lived a bohemian life of poverty and poetry. He was a clerk and dishwasher. He lived in a basement room that would appear frequently in his poems. From 'Background, Casually':

> *Twenty-two: time to go abroad.*
> *First, the decision, then a friend*
> *To pay the fare. Philosophy,*
> *Poverty and Poetry, three*
> *Companions shared my basement room.*

6. In 1952 he returned to India. He worked for passage on a British cargo ship that was taking armaments to Indo-China. The poet Ezekiel scrubbed the decks and hauled coal. At around the same time he was setting sail, London's Fortune Press published his first book and copies awaited him when he disembarked in Bombay. The book was titled *A Time for Change* and it was nothing short of revolutionary for the time.

7. He was the first Indian poet to use contemporary language, without the high-flown style and 19th-century rhetoric that marked the verse of Sarojini Naidu and Aurobindo Ghosh. His tone was ironic, self-mocking, layered with complexities of texture and voice. In a steady progression of books over the next

35 years he would refine that voice, and in the process, teach several generations of Indian poets how to write. He wrote about the city, about sex, about real men and women. In the following lines from 'Poet, Lover, Birdwatcher' he celebrates the importance of patience, especially for the activities described in the title:

> *To force the pace and never to be still*
> *Is not the way of those who study birds*
> *Or women. The best poets wait for words.*

8. In Bombay he joined *The Illustrated Weekly of India* as assistant editor, founded Quest, a cultural and political journal, worked as a copywriter, factory manager, and broadcast journalist, before taking up a professorship at Bombay University.

9. In time he would come to define Bombay as much as the city would define him. It is a looming presence in his poems, a kind of purgatory, or a far circle of hell. He wrote about it without resorting to easy sentimentality, and he sometimes evoked the tormented images of Baudelaire and Dante. From 'A Morning Walk':

> *Barbaric city sick with slums,*
> *Deprived of seasons, blessed with rains,*
> *Its hawkers, beggars, iron-lunged,*
> *Processions led by frantic drums,*
> *A million purgatorial lanes,*
> *and child-like masses, many-tongued*
> *whose wages are in words and crumbs.*

10. If his attitude to Bombay, and to India, was ambivalent, there were also lines that could easily be parodied. He wrote as if he were making fun of himself, of his marginality and outsider status, as in the two concluding lines from this section of 'In India':

Always, in the sun's eye,
Here among the beggars,
Hawkers, pavement sleepers,
Hutment dwellers, slums,
Dead souls of men and gods,
Burnt-out mothers, frightened
Virgins, wasted child
And tortured animal,
All in noisy silence
Suffering the place and time.
I ride my elephant of thought,
A Cezanne slung around my neck.

11. In 1964, V S Naipaul's *An Area of Darkness* (Andre Deutsch, 1964) appeared to unanimous outrage in India. The book's critics said Naipaul had focused on India's poverty, bureaucracy, and lack of hygiene to the exclusion of everything else. Naipaul was obsessed by defecation, said his critics. He was hysterical. The poet Ezekiel became a beacon of sanity in the contentious debate that ensued. His essay, 'Naipaul's India and Mine' was published the following year:

"In the India which I have presumed to call mine, I acknowledge without hesitation the existence of all the darkness Mr. Naipaul has discovered. I am not a Hindu and my background makes me a natural outsider: circumstances and decisions relate me to India. In other countries I am a foreigner. In India I am an Indian... I am incurably critical and skeptical. That is what I am in relation to India also. And to myself. I find it does not prevent the growth of love. In this sense only, I love India. I expect nothing in return because critical, skeptical love does not beget love. It performs another, more objective function."

12. The poet Ezekiel's connection with India was an abiding subject of his verse. His quarrel with Naipaul, he said, arose because 'Mr. Naipaul is so often uninvolved and unconcerned.' Not everybody had Naipaul's choice. For most people, he said, escape was not from the community but into it. A dozen years later, the subject would come up again. Again, from 'Background, Casually':

> *I have made my commitments now.*
> *This is one: to stay where I am.*
> *As others choose to give themselves*
> *In some remote and backward place.*
> *My backward place is where I am.*

13. That day in the restaurant, he asked me why I was leaving India. I replied that I wished to learn how to be a better writer. And I think I made a reference to "this backward place." He stopped eating and for a moment the years dropped from his eyes: they were utterly lucid and clear. "You don't have to go away to learn to write better," he said. "But it may help."

14. Ezekiel was a role model for many writers: not only did he write knowledgeably about art, literature, and theater, he had held jobs in journalism and advertising. I asked him how he moved between poetry and prose with such apparent ease. I wanted to know how he managed to protect his poetry although he wrote so much prose – on deadline, to make a living.

His reply was simplicity itself. He never worked very hard on prose, he said, he just let it write itself. Of course, reading some of his art criticism and essays, this is difficult to believe: they are as well-crafted as his poems. Then he said the words I took with me from that afternoon, words I carry with me still. "I only ever worked hard on a poem," he said.

Kamal Balsara-Bacha

Dear Mrs. M, so thrilled to be included in this prestigious & more than that such a landmark book. I'm writing mainly about you as YOU were instrumental in cultivating my love for poetry and language. And through you I met your wonderful dad.

Serendipity. It's a word I first learned in Mrs. M's AP English class. Since then it has come to define many aspects of my life & the intricate way life threads its way back, almost like a honing device, to the people & places that mattered and who have in some way played an integral role, even if very small in the larger context of things, in your life.

I met Mr. Ezekiel in the late 80's, he had come to visit Mrs. M in Mussoorie where I was a student at Woodstock. She being the ever innovative, generous teacher, had asked him to come talk to our AP English class. My first recollection of him was, he's not as impressive as I thought he'd be. He appeared "old" to me at the age of 17, (youth is unforgiving of anyone with grey hair) and in my mind having imagined Shelley & Byron as these swashbuckling poets, he seemed a little 'tame.'

But what does youth know of experience and gratitude? He sat down, not at the desk, but among us. He asked us to make a circle & then proceeded to ask each one of us what poetry meant to us. That really flummoxed me & I remember giving some pseudo-intellectual half-baked answer, hoping it would not reflect badly on Mrs. M as our teacher.

On that cold wintry day, I think I came to the conclusion that, whilst being profound & having gravity of emotions, poetry does not necessarily have to be serious. You can convey, through the use of humor, your point & at the same time make it relevant. He read to us from his poem, 'The Professor'. His voice was soft but the invocations and the accents had us in splits. His eyes twinkling behind those glasses (he had mischievous eyes – and Mrs. M has them too!), he created an atmosphere that made us feel as if we were there listening to The Professor himself talk about his sons & his life. There was no longer 'him' & 'us'. He came "down", so to speak, to our level. He engaged us, he was intrigued by our stories, this acclaimed poet, was sitting amidst us, listening, chatting with us! It's an experience I shall never forget & the man I had thought "too old to be cool" came to be the epitome of cool & achieved colossal status in all our eyes. He knew how to laugh, how to engage and hold our attention & how important it was, he told us to remember our identity, where we came from, the histories & stories we carried that made us unique and to channel those in our writing.

Some years later as a teacher I had the honor and privilege of teaching his 'Night of the Scorpion' to my 10th grade class. I began the session by telling them I had to be the luckiest person there. I had not only had the privilege of meeting and interacting with him but had in large part become a teacher because of his daughter who I was serendipitously now back in touch with. I have taught some of his other poems to my IB English students, some that encapsulate with such color the local lingo & way of life, and on a deeper level show us human foibles: 'Soap' & 'Farewell for Pushpa TS' being a couple I've taught. And, as serendipity goes, I'm going to be teaching a personal favorite, 'Background, Casually', which I think especially in our world of religious bigotry and fanaticism, rings true. It must be serendipity that Mrs. M asked me to write a few words, because in doing so, I have awakened & relived those wonderful memories of a fleeting youth made all the more memorable because I knew them both.

Menka Shivdasani

One of the greatest joys of a budding writer is the thrill of meeting a 'real live poet' – someone who has crossed the magical path from pen and ink to a printed page; someone so great that you study his or her work in school.

When Nissim Ezekiel was to do a poetry reading, our class at Queen Mary School was told that 15 students could be accommodated. Since we had just studied 'Night of the Scorpion', this seemed like an unbelievable opportunity, and even those who otherwise did not care for poetry decided they wanted to attend. So, lots were drawn, and I proved unlucky! In fact, my classmates even acknowledged that since I was the one most deeply interested in poetry, I should have won a place. They were sympathetic, but not enough to give up a seat.

Then, a year later, straight out of school, and writing prolifically, I had the good fortune of meeting Patanjali Sethi, the then Training Officer of The Times of India. He read my poems and offered to introduce me to someone who was far more "qualified" to judge them. That 'someone' turned out to be Nissim Ezekiel.

Nissim was at the University of Mumbai at Kala Ghoda in those days, and I decided to visit him there, clutching the precious letter that Patanjali Sethi had given me, along with a few poems in my best handwriting. I also wanted him to take me seriously, so, all of sixteen years old, I wore a saree.

Seated behind what seemed like a huge desk in a gigantic room, Nissim was surprised, but gracious, when I walked in. He read the letter, glanced at the poems, and tossed them back across his desk. "Type them," he said. "You can't judge a poem unless it is typed." I thought it was his way of getting rid of this young girl wasting his time, so I thanked him, and moved to the door. "Wait," he said and asked me to write down my name and number. I did so, and left, vowing never to return. Then two weeks later, he called. "You were going to come back with your poems," he said. "What happened?"

Over the next several years, we met regularly, at least once a week; our fixed day was Wednesday, 10 a.m., and once, since we hadn't confirmed this during the previous meeting and I didn't show up, he called to remind me.

It was through Nissim, at this transformational stage of my life, that I met many of the poets who were making their presence felt as contemporary writers in India – though strangely, I never did meet his daughter Kavita, from the same school as me. "She's also a poet," he told me on multiple occasions with pride.

It was through Nissim that I learned the importance of craft, the value of finding one's voice as a writer, and the most fundamental lesson of all – that no matter how high one goes in life, one must always aim higher.

As I got to know him better, I realized that this was someone who truly cared about nurturing good poetry, who was generous with his time and advice when he thought someone had potential. I think people sometimes took this for granted. I remember a teenaged boy once walking into the PEN office and demanding to know if Nissim had read his manuscript. Nissim sheepishly mumbled that he hadn't been able to do so, only to be angrily told – "But you've had it for a month!" Instead of throwing him out, Nissim apologized and promised to look at it as soon as possible.

This humility extended to his own poetry; he was as willing to listen to feedback as he was to give it. When he wrote his Nudes series, he said he wouldn't show me his work because it would shock me; I was, after all, barely seventeen. I insisted he do so, and when he reluctantly shared the poems, I did not convey that I was, indeed, shocked; instead, I told him he had missed a comma in the third line. Nissim laughed uproariously. "You've learned my lessons too well, you so-and-so!" he declared.

Once, he handed me a proof of a poem by him that some journal wanted to publish and asked if I could help him with it.

It was the very same one I had learned in school, 'Night of the Scorpion'. "I can't bear to look at it," he said. "Everyone seems to think it is the only poem I have written!"

My own personal favorite Nissim poem was 'Poet, Lover, Birdwatcher'. I thought it was amazing how he brought the three entities together so seamlessly. I also remind myself, in this age when people seem to be writing what they refer to as poetry at the drop of a hat, that "the best poets wait for words".

One of my most painful memories of Nissim was about two decades after I first met him when I offered to drop him home, and he could not remember the name of the house in which he had lived for so many years or the street on which it was. In the end, after we had circled past the chaotic traffic outside Bombay Central station at peak hours five or six times, he suggested I just drop him off there; his legs would automatically take him home, he said. It was the first sign I had that something was very wrong. When he was eventually hospitalized, I met him a few times, though a stage arrived when he no longer recognized me.

Today, decades later, when I speak to youngsters about writing poetry, I reference Nissim Ezekiel and the many things I learned from him about the craft, and even about attitudes to life when I was their age – about always aiming higher, never becoming complacent, and continuing to write, no matter what the challenges may be.

Mohana Rao

The Shimmering Midnight Sky: a distinct rhythmic sound crescendos, silencing the familiar nocturnal recital of the nightcrawlers. The sound of a scribbling ballpoint flowing over the linear grey path of a notebook, flickering flames of a candle, synchronized with the glittering sparkle of the stars brightening the ebony Himalayan skies, setting the stage for a lone poet fighting his fatigue to compose his immortal verse, concluding his poem by juxtaposing two shining teenage stars against the greying man on the moon. The man who today through his lyrical artistry is the glistening star, he once scribed late into the night under the shimmering midnight sky.

Picture of Mohana and Olinda (in the scarf) the 'two stars' of Nissim Ezekiel's poem 'Lost and Found in Mussoorie.'

Olinda Belt

It may not have been a star-filled night, but how were we to know the tall, polite gentleman who approached us would bring to it a treasured memory of stars captured in a poem for eternity. Mr. Ezekiel introduced himself to us, looking for directions to his daughter Mrs. Mendonca's home. My friend Mohana and I didn't have to think twice, he was automatically part of the Woodstock family even if only by association to our well-loved teacher. I don't remember the exact conversation we had, but I do remember the lightheartedness of the evening, suitcase in hand, making our way up the uneven, winding paths typical of the Mussoorie hillside.

I distinctly remember my astonishment when he read the poem he had written about us, the next day at our high school assembly in Parker Hall. I slid down a little lower in my seat, a little embarrassed by the attention, but inwardly glowing at this first poem ever written for me. I was also a little in awe at his talent, for he had captured a moment in time so beautifully.

It is perhaps for this reason that I have carried this treasured, handwritten piece of poetry to twelve different cities, three different continents and numerous different homes. This was an effortlessly written piece of poetry by Mr. Ezekiel, but for me a little bit of the past captured and preserved. Each time I open my file of special memories, I come across this poem and there it is – a memory of a dark night that conjures up stars that bring a smile to my day.

Lost and Found in Mussoorie

Lost and Found in Mussoorie
(For Olinda and Mohana)

The taxi-driver blew his own horn
in more senses than one,
but could not find the place
The moon did not help
but two stars did.
One had a torch, the other
carried my luggage with a smile.
Their voices warmed the chilly air—
stars can be musical!
I shall remember both
now and forever,
sweet fifteen today:
stay sweet, my dear stars, for ever.

22/Sept/85   NISSIM EZEKIEL

Nissim Ezekiel
18 Kala Niketan
47-C Bhulabhai Desai Road
Bombay 400 026

This copy for Olinda. K.

Copyright in the poem: The Estate of Nissim Ezekiel
(Poem sent in by Olinda Belt)

Raul Da Gama Rose
Responses to questions from Kavita Ezekiel Mendonca

I am going to answer these questions without guile. Some of what I say may sound blunt, but I am attempting to be as honest as I can. This is the only way I know. It helps that I have a photographic memory and remember things like colors of clothes, backgrounds, and things like that. As you probably know, the year was 1973... I was young and impressionable, and a bit hot-headed too. I knew I wanted to write poetry by the time I was 12 or 13 – i.e., 1960 or 61. But I knew less about Indian writers than I did the European ones – English, Scottish, Welsh, Irish – and the Portuguese [my first language] ones. By the time I knew Indian writing in English Joseph Furtado [who wrote primarily in Portuguese] and Armando Menezes and Dom Moraes were three of the only four Indian writers I knew. The fourth one was your father. I was in awe of him when Adil introduced me to his writing... but being the kind of hot-headed and opinionated person that I was at that age, I was difficult to handle and– to use an Americanism – shot from the hip, mostly without really thinking.

Anyway, I hope that this preface does not give you the wrong impression of me. I only mean to record the events as I remember as [vividly as] they happened. You may edit them however you think fit.

Seven Questions on Nissim Ezekiel

1. When did you first meet my father, Nissim Ezekiel? Do you remember anything specific or special associated with that first encounter? Further encounters?
My first meeting with Nissim Ezekiel was at his office at the University of Bombay. This was in June of 1973. It was pouring. I wore my hair long in those days, dressed in a kurta and jeans

– a sign that I felt European [my father is Brazilian and my mum a mix of Indian and Persian], but was trying to "belong" somewhere – India, at that time. I couldn't understand why I needed to "belong" to India but writing in English in India felt dissonant. Anyway...

Nissim was dressed in a yellow shirt with a tiny floral pattern; a bush-shirt that he wore outside his pants [I came to realize this was characteristic of him]. He was serious but looked kind. He shook my hand and asked me to sit. There was another person in the room with him.

I was already intimidated at being in the presence of a poet who was at the pinnacle of his career and felt that somehow things were going to go down like a lead balloon. Anyway, I plucked up the courage to speak to your dad.

So pulling out a sheaf of paper from my "bagal-thaila" (I think that's what you called those cloth shoulder bags we all carried in those days). Looking at the other person in the room, I put the poems in front of Nissim. He read the first one without any change in his expression; then the second and the third. They were all short poems. Then he said: "Well, Raul, that's good. But what do you want to achieve as a writer?"

"I want to be like John Keats," I replied. I had the romantic notion that I would write poems like 'Ode to a Grecian Urn' and 'Endymion', contract T.B. by the time I was 27, and die of it. I didn't make that confession to Nissim, but I think he got the feeling that I was a poet-in-a-hurry. He looked me straight in the eye and said: "These works are a good beginning," he said, "But if you want to be like Keats, you'll have to put in a lot more work. Keats wrote hundreds of poems before he wrote the "right" ones... before he could be recognized..." he said.

I am not sure what I wanted to hear from Nissim about my work. He asked me where I was studying, who my teachers were. I named Eunice De Souza and Adil. "You're in good hands," he said, enigmatically.

The next day I reported this to Adil, who had set the whole thing up. Adil calmed me down. He said, "Well... Nissim is right...If you want to emulate Keats, you'll have to work really hard at your work," he opined. I thought hard about Nissim's advice about "working" on my poems.

There were several encounters at Samovar, and at a South Indian restaurant on a Marine Lines. We became much friendlier as our encounters multiplied. I kept filling him in with what I was up to, and two years later, when Santan Rodrigues, Melanie Silgardo and I founded *Newground*, and published our book *3 Poets*, I gave him a copy. This time he had a BIG smile on his face. He promised to read the poems, put his hand around me and said, "Keats..." Then he smiled a big smile and left.

2. What were your impressions of my father? How did these change, as you got to know him better?

I felt that Nissim was a kind man. I could see that in his face. But I also knew that he was a demanding artist. After all he didn't get there by dashing off the first things that came to his mind. At a subsequent meeting he told me, "The gift of writing makes you an artist, but you have to develop the attitude of a craftsman. And you can only do that if you work at the gift... chip away at the extra bits, trim the rough edges... chisel away at the words... fine-tune the idiom...craftsmanship is just as important to the artist as being aware of the art itself."

I felt close to him after meeting – and eating at the table with him. I stopped feeling alone even though there were times when nothing much was said... somehow I felt that everything that mattered was understood.

3. Can you describe him in his professional work, such as writing, mentoring younger poets, art critic, working at the PEN?

Nissim and Adil were the only mentors I had...have... When I have a problem expressing a metaphor, my urge is to go back to their work, or a conversation we may have had, to find a way to smooth the rough edges of my own work. Adil fed my artistic fire... Nissim not only fed that fire, but he taught me how to stoke the fire. I later realized that he had worked on board a ship. Our bond grew exponentially after that because my own father sailed supply ships during World War II...After that we found many more things to talk about. But every time we met, no matter what we talked about, he always had a tip about writing to share with me...he told me to watch out for glibness and trite imagery... "You have a gift for writing," he used to say, "Writing comes easily to you, but beware of the things that come to you easily," he said.

I attended all of his P.E.N. lectures and other programs. I devoured his art criticism and, in many ways, I grew to appreciate Sabavala, Anjolie Ela Menon and others purely on the basis of his art criticism.

But by far, my favourite work of criticism of your dad's was the essay, "Naipaul's India and Mine". It is a work on par with anything George Steiner or Susan Sontag or Auden have written... the greatest rebuttal to Naipaul by anyone anywhere in the world... including Paul Theroux.

I don't think that I am alone in glorifying Nissim for all the things you have asked me. Santan and I used to speak a lot about how much he meant to the poets of our generation... Later he consented to be guest editor of *Kavi*. It was an enormous honor for us, but that was Nissim... generous to a fault, someone who gave of himself completely...

4. Do you have an anecdote that you would consider sharing?
I was part of the group that was at that restaurant when Nissim found that bug in his food... you know the rest. It was typical of his gentleness... and about being generous to a fault.

5. What is your favorite poem of my father's?

You're putting me on the spot here... It's hard to single out a "favorite poem"...I have several, but for brevity's sake I'll say 'Night of the Scorpion', 'Background Casually', and if I may, everything in *Latter Day Psalms*.

6. Do you have any memories of me with my father, on any occasion?

Just one... I saw you with him once at the Jehangir Art Gallery. He introduced you to me. I couldn't get over how alike you looked. You still smile the same way and, every time I look at photographs of you, I remember him. I thought how fortunate you were to have him as a father. Later, I learned you have a brother too – Elkana – who I believe had something to do with drama.

7. Is there anything else you would like to add?

I still read Nissim's work, not simply to enjoy his poetry, but often to learn how to resolve a thought in danger of overtaking the heart of an emotion. "Night of the Scorpion" is a classic example as is everything in *Latter Day Psalms*. He is also a master of how to prune a line... to distil it to the essence of an emotion... how to strengthen and chisel [his word] an image; to make it "everything" to the poem.

Saleem Peeradina
A Poet, Rascal, Clown, Speaks

Express Magazine 1986

Since he started writing and publishing in the early fifties, Nissim Ezekiel has been widely acknowledged as the father of modern Indian poetry in English. Today, he could well be regarded as the granddad of them all – the two generations of poets who have followed him, some of whom he nurtured and groomed, others who found in him a father figure to rebel against.

Although 20 years hence, the prospect of being labelled the grand old man of poetry might seem somewhat debilitating to him, there is no doubt that Ezekiel's contribution to the development of Indian poetry, and to the cultural scene in general, will be seen as a formative one.

One of my first meetings with him – nearly 30 years ago – was in a garage, which used to serve as the Imprint office, in the compound of a building in south Bombay. I had taken some of my poems to him to see if he could use them in Poetry India – at that time the only classy poetry magazine in the country. (Curiously, there is very little since then to match that short-lived venture.) I remember how encouraging Ezekiel was, how helpful in his criticism, how earnest in the total attention he gave me in those few moments. I was thrilled to bits – I was still an undergraduate then – when he decided to publish three of my poems in his magazine. One of the roles that Ezekiel has played all his life, with the grace and honesty that have always been his mark, is to put the subjectivity of new writers in a proper frame of reference.

Sometime later, a mild shock was to come with my discovery of "The Retreat", Ezekiel's family home. For many of us it was not just an ordinary address then, it was a place of historical interest. I imagined it to be a cozy cottage full of books, antique furniture, etchings on the wall, tastefully furnished, color-coordinated with sensuous textures – in short, an aesthetic treat. After all, Ezekiel was the art critic of the time. It turned out to be an old, run-down house with very modest living quarters, with no evidence of an ordering hand – the most functional furniture, bare stone floor, a cot with a regulation bedcover, an open mori with bucket, *matka* (large earthenware pot) and a *lota* (a medium-sized roundish vessel, sometimes with a spout).

So art and life – or rather art theory and personal taste – didn't mix. In the PEN office, which Ezekiel has been using for many years as editor of the PEN newsletter, one notices the same disinterest in the aesthetics of the interior space that the man occupies. Form and content lie in total disarray, with the lord of the mess sitting at peace within it. But one soon feels at home among the dusty books and files, typescripts of poems, loose sheets of paper, journals of Commonwealth origin, paper-weighted letters, more magazines stacked on a chair, more loose sheets spilling out of a rotting briefcase, assorted odds and ends strewn on the table, back issues of PEN lying like stagnant drain water on the floor, neatly filed, post-ready issues of the current newsletter, piles of other stuff leaning dangerously from the top of a cupboard, a broken table fan wrapped in a gunny bag waiting for its burial – each object left to its own device, living its prescribed fate.

There is a story about Ezekiel's spectacles, which he had been wearing for 25 years and which he had only recently exchanged for a similar, brand-new pair. The old ones tilted precariously on the bridge of his Jewish nose, their glass surface smudged and scratched, their rivets caked with the rust of a quarter-century. This was the pair that Ebrahim Alkazi, an old friend and Ezekiel's contemporary in the theatre, had found for him, escorting him to the oculist. Since then, chaperoning him to outfit him with personal effects has become the burden of friends. (In one of his poems, an admirer-lover sends him a gift of new underclothes but prefers to have him wear his old, worn-out ones for their own rendezvous.) More than a dozen of his concerned friends, lovers, well-wishers must have badgered Ezekiel on different occasions to have his spectacles replaced. But like an obstinate child, he insisted he wanted a rimless pair which looked exactly like the old one. Finally, a newly acquired friend-patron bodily dragged him to a shop he know and fished out a gleaming new pair that seemed to satisfy Ezekiel's finicky taste. Henceforth, all gift items will have to exclude spectacles. For the next quarter century, the poet is not going to need another pair!

In 1985, Nissim Ezekiel officially retired from his position of Reader in English at Bombay University, which concluded a 25-year teaching career. He came late but stayed on the longest. What many people do not know is that in addition to teaching and writing and being a magazine-editor and art critic, Ezekiel has tried his hand at a whole lot of short-lived occupations – starting as a copywriter in a Bombay ad agency, moving up as a manager in the same outfit, doing a stint as a journalist in *The Illustrated Weekly*, serving as a manager for Chemould, a frame-manufacturing concern where he juggled his time and wrote *The Unfinished Man*, his fourth book of poems, then switching to Imprint as editor.

But to begin at the beginning…

When did you first decide you were going to be a poet?
At a very early age. I was always interested in poetry. I generally read more than my classmates. Even as a 10-year-old, I preferred reading poetry to prose, which was quite unusual in my class, even among the best students. I was never really interested in subjects like mathematics and geography as many others were – these were considered to be the "scoring" subjects. I was thought to be a bit of an eccentric.

What were your early attempts at poetry like? Did you have a mentor? Did you model yourself on any great writer or poet?
I modelled myself on the poets that are normally read in India in school textbooks – Shelley, Byron, Keats, and others. I couldn't possibly have had any other models. The Inspiration did not come as much from the poets as from my teachers. In Antonio D'Souza High School there were a number of poetry enthusiasts and some of them read poetry in the classroom loudly and clearly – very rhythmically, in fact, and I used to feel quite thrilled listening to them.

Did you start publishing right after you left school?
Publishing came later. When I was at college, I sent a poem of mine to a political magazine – I think it was a weekly being edited by K. M. Munshi. I used to buy this magazine regularly for political reasons – this was in early 1942. Of course, as often happens in India, there was no acknowledgement from the journal – but the poem was published, and that's what mattered. I bought a large number of copies myself. Subsequently, I started sending out poems to various magazines all over India.

Were you bothered about whether your poetry would be read at all, whether people would respond to it?
These questions did not really arise in my mind – the question of the audience, whether poetry is read, what it means to write in English, whether Indian poetry in English has an audience, these and other similar questions did not trouble me at all. At that stage, it was only important to read poetry, to write poetry, to read about poetry, and if possible, to meet one or two friends and discuss poetry. It was too subjective a thing. It didn't become "intellectual" till much later. It was in my early 20s that it became formulated as a kind of vocation, a career. By that time I had written a fairly large amount. In fact, that is one thing I can always say about myself, I've written a lot.

I cannot say anything about the quality of my writing – 200 recent poems, there they are. How good the 200 are, and how many of them really deserve to be published – all these are secondary questions for me. I don't think of individual poems in that sense. I am inclined to write as much as possible and then work on these drafts much later – sometimes I link them together, revise them, improve them.

When did your first book come out?
In 1952, in London, published by The Fortune Press. I didn't know at that time that it was a "vanity press". I simply saw a number of copies containing poems by a young English poet. I saw an advertisement and wrote a letter to the publisher saying that I had a manuscript ready. I got a reply saying that he was willing to publish my poems. He came to my basement room in London. He told me that he would publish my manuscript, if I paid for the printing. The cost would be around $10. I told him that $10 is what I would need to live for five weeks, and I couldn't possibly raise the amount. I told him that he could publish the poems if he liked them, or just forget them. And we parted on that note.

Later, I told my roommate, Krishna Paigankar, what had happened. He said, "Nonsense, you cannot postpone the publication of your book for the sake of $10." He gave me the $10. I wrote to the publisher again and sent the $10 and my manuscript. The book, however, came out after I had left London.

What was your objective in going to London? Did you set out on some sort of adventure, or did you go to study?
I was very confused, I must say. I really didn't know what I was going for. To some, I said I was going to study art in Paris, to others I said I was going to study philosophy in London. There were a series of contradictory answers I always had ready for use. Eventually, I went to London and started looking out for a

job, and within two or three months, I got one at India House. I arrived in October 1948 and left in May 1952.

What did you do after coming back?
There was actually a job for me in Bombay. One of the persons in India who knew of my problems and disappointments in London was C. R. Mandy of the *Illustrated Weekly*. He wrote me a letter saying that if I sent him my poems, he would publish them and if I ever returned to India, I could join the editorial staff of the journal. I did that. My friend, Alkazi, as witty as ever, said, on hearing of it: "You set out to be illustrious and ended up being illustrated."

I subsequently left the *Weekly* to join Shilpi. I didn't know it was an advertising concern. They advertised for a person capable of writing good English – and I thought I was at least capable of that. I was appointed and was asked to write a script for an advertising film. I stayed on for five years. In between, I was sent to New York and elsewhere in America to study advertising. Whether I learnt much about it I am not going to confess.

I left Shilpi in 1958, and for one year I was with Kekoo Gandhi, and his factory at Andheri. I was factory manager there and it was in the factory that I wrote *The Unfinished Man*. In fact, I began to write it because I looked into the factory itself and found that if you organize things properly in a factory you have some spare time to read and write. Then arose the thought of going back to teaching (I had done a couple of stints earlier). My sustained teaching career began in 1961.

Your Jewishness never seems to intrude in any implicit or explicit manner in your writing, except for some direct references in some poems. Why is this?
Partly because at the age of 18 or 19 I had moved away not only from Judaism, but from all religion. I had become atheistic and anti-religious, and it was a fairly long spell. I always loved

mysticism, however. But it was mysticism as poetry rather than as religion.

You went through an LSD phase? Have you left that behind? Did it make any impression on your work or life?
It didn't leave a mark on my writing. In fact, that was one of the disappointments of the LSD experience. But it left a great impression on me as a person for the simple reason that with the first LSD experience, I gave up atheism – it just collapsed. Religion and its mysteries became more acceptable. A number of things happened to me which were very important and still are. I didn't continue to take LSD because if you take a drug over a period of time you experience both its positive and negative effects. It became clear to me that I couldn't continue to use LSD regularly. I was very strict and disciplined in my use of it. I took exactly the lowest dosage that was recommended by the experts. The first experience was in 1967 and I continued taking it till 1970.

Have there been any conflicts between your work life, your writing life and your personal life? How constructive or destructive have they been to your writing?
I've never felt there was a discord, because when I'm doing the other things, I feel I am living, I am working, I am relating to people. I am responding to the situations around me. I never feel that I want to get away from all this "discord" and have a little bungalow in Matheran, where I can stay by myself and enjoy its scenic beauty. On the other hand, to say that there is perfect harmony between my writing life and other life is too much of a claim to make. From time to time, I do cross the line. I live and enjoy my work, and at some stage, feel that I am losing contact with the written word altogether. When that happens, I try to retreat, and restore the balance a little bit. Then something may get written, good, satisfactory things may get written. Again, the

logic of events pulls me back to the world and I stop writing and so that pull, back and forth, goes on and has been going on for the last 35 years.

Have you had any serious crises in your writing career? If so, how have you coped with them?
No, I have never had a full-scale block. I have always written prodigiously. Whether what I wrote was good or bad or indifferent never mattered at the time of writing. I wrote because I enjoyed it. Sometimes, a bad poem can lead to a good one. Certain ideas occur when you are writing bad poems out of which a good poem could emerge. Since that was my method, I never really had what can be called a total "block". But in the last year or so, I have not really written much poetry. I discovered a story of mine written in 1951 in London, which had never been published. I didn't have to revise it very much, only change a word or two. I sent it to a Commonwealth literature journal published in Denmark. It was promptly accepted and published. It has given me a great boost. And I want to write more short stories.

Do you think you have made a successful literary career in India? Maybe you could have got greater recognition abroad.
I don't think so. I've met many Indian writers abroad, and 99 per cent of them disappear into the void because they are misinterpreted and underestimated. If you decide you are an exile, you can make something of it. If you try to get into the mainstream, then your chances of making it are very weak. I think I would be an odd man out anywhere else. If I have to be an odd man out, then I would prefer being one here. Even now people ask me, now that you have retired, would you like to settle abroad? That's the last thing I want to do. I don't want to leave even Bombay, for that matter. All my writing comes out of staying here. I am happy to be unhappy here rather than somewhere else. If I stay anywhere else, I will only be unhappy. Here, at

least the unhappiness makes sense, unhappiness lead to critical perceptions. One can take a positive approach to frustration or a negative one. I certainly take the positive approach. It is more creative. If any work of mine does not get the recognition I think it deserves, I'm not unduly upset. Some people push and pull and attempt to promote their work. But I cannot spend all my time trying to get recognition. I've got to do some writing as well.

What have you meant your poetry to achieve?
If a poem is above all a poem, it cannot have any other form, it cannot exist as a prose summary of it, then it is an achievement as a poem. There is a certain sense of the inevitable in a real poem. It cannot stand for something else. It has to be what it is. If I have written 60 poems in the last five years, I know that 45 of them won't have this sort of inevitability. That is what I demand of a poem. It should be unconditionally a poem, and only a poem.

Do you think that poets in India have stretched their resources to the maximum?
The performance of most Indian poets in English is comparable to the performance of our athletes in the Olympics.

How would you advise young and up-and-coming poets to go about their work?
A certain amount of critical reading is always good. Writing poetry without reading all the outstanding advice given by outstanding critics about poetry is like climbing a mountain without a guide and without any equipment. You are likely to come down with a bump. Reading disciplines one's art. Of course, the case of the genius or the wild man is different. He may get his inspiration from some mad, mysterious source and translate it into magnificent, disciplined art subconsciously. But in normal cases, some sort of critical reading is a must, and any attempt to be naïve there is dangerous. This does not imply that a poet

must accept everything he reads. A good poet allows himself to be influenced, assimilates the influence, resists the influence. For a good poet, influence does not mean imitation, it can even mean going in the opposite direction. A poet can read and appreciate fantastically free poetry and yet when it comes to himself, he may write in just the opposite way – very controlled, taut, rhymed stanza forms.

Don't you think that the Indian cultural ethos is fundamentally discouraging, and sometimes even disruptive, to creativity?
Well, I have always taken it as a bit of a joke rather than seriously. After saying things like poetry has no future, you go around the world because you have written poetry. The primary question is related to poetry as a vocation, whether it can be a vocation at all or does it only remain at the level of a hobby. I don't understand these people who are afraid of criticism and run away from it by saying that "I only write for myself; it is my hobby." I think that is running away from the problem. I'm not upset by any popular notion of what poetry should be like.

John Berryman once joked that an assistant professor could become an associate professor by working on his senior's poetry. How do you feel about being the subject of a Ph.D. thesis?
I am supposed to feel flattered. Actually, there are ways of looking at it, and both of them go together. One way is to take it lightly, joke about it before others can do the same. And I don't ever give up that way of looking at it. On the other hand, one has to be fair to the person doing the work and one has to be consistent. I have given a lot of thought to these things, and then followed the logic of a central decision. For example, if I receive a letter from someone saying I want to register for my Ph.D. and the letter does not contain a single sentence of correct English, I'll be very firm and say that there are some qualifications that are indispensable, and you don't have them.

So, sorry, I can't help you. He may be upset about it, but I have to be a little firm.

On the other hand, if there is this man who does his work and then comes to you for some more material, you cannot refuse to help him. But ultimately, it ends up with you doing research on yourself. This can get a bit out of hand – and, at some stage, you must set the limits. If the student, for instance, is trying to trace an article on me that appeared in *The Statesman* in 1947, and comes to me for it, I will advise him right away to go to *The Statesman* office and find out.

How do you feel about your retirement? For most people it is an arbitrary thing that is forced upon them. I am sure you have a very active life ahead of you.
Mine is definitely not a retirement in any conventional sense. I have seen people retire and then ask others what they should do. This question never arose in my mind. I've always had plenty to do. In fact, my wife complains that now I work as much as I ever did when I was teaching. When you have more time to write than when you were teaching full-time, you tend to spend more time working on each draft. So, I have plenty to do. I am more bothered about finding what not to do, because sometimes things do get out of hand.

You have an extraordinary ability to write under any circumstances. I'm told a minor domestic storm may be raging at the dining table, and you are scribbling away.
Actually, that was a decision I took in opposition to the attitude of some of my friends that they, too, would be writers "on condition that" – and I know that if I made conditions like that, I would not be a writer at all. At least one person has been saying for 25 years that if he gets a quiet room to write in, he would write. I haven't got my quiet room and I hope I have become a writer. He hasn't got his quiet room and he hasn't become a writer. I am

afraid of making excuses. I'd rather struggle and admit, perhaps, that under ideal conditions, the writing would have been better. But the quiet room is not indispensable. To crave for it is self-defeating and I can't stand self-defeating attitudes, from others and from myself. I feel I must take the responsibility and say that I did my best in my circumstances.

Salil Tripathi

Nissim used to eat lunch every day at Sanman, a restaurant next to the American Center, the American library in Bombay. I knew him as a college student (I studied at Sydenham, which was nearby). And during those long summer months from March to May, when we went daily to the library to revise our coursework in the weeks leading up to our university exams, some of us would go to Sanman for lunch. (Sanman used to make better *sambar* than Satkar, which was closer to Sydenham).

I would meet Nissim often then – he had read my early poems, and we often talked about literature. If my staple diet was *idli-sambar*, his was boiled vegetables with mayonnaise.

One day, he was seated at the table next to ours, and we greeted each other – I was with a bunch of classmates, and we were probably discussing the film to see that evening, instead of some calculus problem baffling us. I saw some activity around Nissim's table. It turns out, along with Nissim's boiled vegetables, the plate included a caterpillar. Nissim wanted to send the plate back.

He did this politely, without making any fuss, without alarming other patrons, realizing this was an accident – Nissim ate there daily for decades – and he had a long, symbiotic relationship with Sanman. When we looked at him silently, the plate having been taken away, Nissim winked at me, smiled, and said: "It was a very hungry caterpillar."

To see humor in something that would outrage any other patron, to be forgiving of an obvious mistake, and not to make any fuss – this little incident is quintessential Ezekiel.

But he could be sarcastic when he wanted to! In late 1980s, I went to interview him (I was a correspondent with *India Today* and writing a piece on the novel-writing boom in India – Penguin had set up shop, and new writers were emerging from everywhere). I asked him what he thought of that. And he said:

"There are novelists and there are people who write novels."

He did not have to say more.

A poet always, a clown – gentle, and sometimes – but never a rascal. I miss Nissim.

Shalva Weil

(Photo credit: Shalva Weil)

I first met Nissim Ezekiel in Bombay. I already had a doctorate in anthropology (D.Phil. from the University of Sussex, UK) after conducting 3 years' fieldwork among the Bene Israel in Lod, Israel. Sara Ezekiel, a senior member of the Bene Israel community, had adopted me as a grandmother and referred me to Nissim since they were friendly from the Jewish Religious Union. Nissim was very much into that non-orthodox, Reform/Liberal type of Judaism with prayers in English. So, it was early in the 1980s that I met your father, and also visited your home and met your mother. She was more traditional. I often wondered how she managed to live with some of his poems. I met him several times in Bombay after that, when I visited the Bene Israel community for follow-up research, until he came to Israel in 1995. My impressions of your father never changed. He was always warm, intelligent, fun, witty and irreverent.

Of course, Nissim wasn't only a poet. I followed his development avidly. He was a playwright, a reviewer and more. Since my major interest was Nissim as a Bene Israel, my favourite poem was and is 'Jewish Wedding in Bombay' with references to Jewish law and custom, as well as real insights into ceremonies and what we call "love". However, today I realise one has to view Nissim in wider perspective against the backdrop of the evolving Bombay cultural scene. I met some of his friends from the Bombay Progressive Artists group. They were all ex-Bohemians, rebels and multi-faceted. So, while Nissim could feel comfortable in the synagogue and at the same time uncomfortable, so too he sat on the margins of some of the greatest artistic episodes and artists that India has produced. Today, in Jerusalem, you are greeted by a wall mural painted by F. N. Souza's grandson, Solomon, a young graffiti artist, who painted a portrait of Nissim on a shutter in the Mahane Yehuda market at my request. It is my way of memorializing Nissim. I tell Solomon about Nissim, and we have found photos of them together.

Nissim's visit to Jerusalem in June 1995 was a personal tribute to me. Everyone said he wouldn't accept my invitation, but I knew he would. At the time, I was Chairperson of the India-Israel Cultural Association (with Zubin Mehta as President) founded in 1992 after diplomatic relations were established between the two countries that year. It was the official friendship association between India and Israel, but I and my committee preferred to focus upon culture rather than commerce and defence, as today. I asked the Israeli Ministry of Foreign Affairs to invite Nissim and pay for his air ticket and accommodation at Mishkenot Sha'ananim in Jerusalem, where international literary stars are hosted. He stayed in those beautiful surroundings opposite the walls of the Old City, and it was there that we held a well-attended poetry reading. After I opened the meeting, the Israeli poet Amir Or introduced him. Some of my committee members knew Shimon Peres, who was a great admirer of Nissim Ezekiel. We organised a reception with Peres, which thrilled Nissim, and also Shimon Peres, and Nissim read out one or two of his poems. One of his poems was translated into Hebrew by the famous Israeli poetess Ruth Almog and appeared on the front page of the weekend cultural supplement of the *Haaretz* newspaper. Then Nissim moved to my residence in Jerusalem. We held another poetry reading for the members of the Indian Jewish community in Lod, where I had lived doing my fieldwork among the community in the 1970s. It was during Nissim's visit to Jerusalem that we realised fully that he was suffering from early Alzheimer's. This must have been Nissim's last foray abroad. He was anyway itching to return to Bombay, the city of his love and his dreams.

Shanta Acharya

As a young poet in Cuttack, Orissa, one grew up hearing of Professor Nissim Ezekiel, the father of post-independence Indian poetry in English. *Time to Change* and *Sixty Poems*, his first two poetry collections, had appeared before I was born. Neither copy was available in our college library. Considering *Time to Change* was published in London, getting hold of a copy in Orissa would have been difficult. Perhaps it was the inaccessibility and the remoteness one experienced in Cuttack that conjured a sense of unreality. It felt like a dream come true when my poem 'Caligula' was published by Nissim Ezekiel in the September-October 1978 issue of the *Journal of the Indian P.E.N.* This was possibly my first outing in a major poetry journal in India though my poems had been published in the Ravenshaw College journal under the editorship of Prof Sarbeswar Dash, Jayanta Mahapatra among others, and I had also have poems accepted in various other Indian magazines.

However, publication in the *Indian P.E.N.* seemed like a miracle of sorts as I had sent my poems without any hope of an acknowledgement, let alone publication. Taking into account the erratic postal service and mysteries of the publishing world, I had no great expectations. Imagine my surprise when a reply arrived within a week! Signed by Nissim Ezekiel, it said my poem 'Caligula' would appear in the forthcoming issue, and the others would appear in subsequent issues. That is how I 'met' Nissim Ezekiel. A notable poet and editor, his acceptance of my work gave me the confidence I needed as a young poet. Over the years, he published several more of my poems.

When I came to Oxford, I valued his almost pastoral support as he urged me to be open to new experiences in life. I did not know anyone in Oxford and the first year is often the bleakest. We kept in touch I kept sending him poems. By the time we met in 1993, Nissim was a friend cum mentor. I was working with

POETS, FRIENDS, STUDENTS AND FAMILY REMEMBER...

Baring Asset Management at the time and my work took me to various places in India, including Bombay. I used to stay at the Taj, courtesy of my employers. The first time I invited him to the Taj with a view to having dinner, he was so appalled by the prices he refused to have anything even after I explained to him that I would not be paying and that he would be doing me a favor as my personal expense bills were so meagre my work colleagues hated me for my frugality. Like Nissim, I too found the prices stratospheric. We went out to a place he knew and had a delicious dinner there. Thankfully, Nissim allowed me to pay. His refusal to eat at the Taj. impressed me, reminded me of my grandparents and parents who would have done the same.

Once he invited me to do a poetry reading at The Theosophy Hall in Bombay, where the *Indian P.E.N. All India Centre* was based. Nissim was generous enough to ask me to read to him first, like a rehearsal. He told me how important it is to project one's voice, reading slowly and clearly, giving each word its due – advice worth sharing.

When my first collection of poems, *Not This, Not That*, appeared in 1994, he was generous enough to endorse it. Nissim's endorsement appears on the cover of *Imagine*, my new and selected poems, which was published by HarperCollins in 2017. It would have been a joy to have been able to present him a copy. I cannot recall when we lost touch, as he fell ill, was unable to write, and my life took many wrong turns. Without his first letter of acceptance, my life and work would not have been the same. He, along with a few other poet-editors in India, including Kamala Das, gave me the confidence as a poet and writer that I continue to cherish.

The Oxford/ England I came to in 1979 was such a different place that the younger generation today may struggle to imagine. While my professors were hugely supportive (John Bayley liked my poems enough to send them to the editor of a well-known journal in London), the world of poetry was a closed arena. The editor of the journal to whom Prof Bayley sent my poems never published any. On another occasion, my poems were rejected with a cryptic message: "But, do you write like Geoffrey Hill?". Though I admire some of his writing, I never understood why I was expected to write like Hill. Nissim, along with Prof Carlo Coppola, who was then editor of the *Journal of South Asian Literature* in the USA, encouraged me to ignore such ignorance. The world of poetry today is still largely closed and remains equally cliquey.

Nissim's poetry is both educational and entertaining. I believe the aim of poetry is to enlighten and entertain. When reading his poems, one can feel the pleasure Nissim took in writing poetry. Like Yeats, he treated poetry as the 'record of the mind's growth,' which is how I came to poetry. It was and still is for me a subversive and solitary activity as much as a way of reaching out to the world. There are so many of Nissim's poems I love and admire that choosing one would be depriving myself of a veritable feast.

Subodh Deshpande
I Lost My Nissim Ezekiel

I lost my Nissim Ezekiel in
a hotel lobby in Istanbul
I was on the edge of discovery
That bit where he talks about
writing good poetry
My enlightenment deficient
My halo incomplete
like a half-eaten donut
I feel like:
...my mentor turned his back on me
...I gave up tennis just as I was
mastering my backhand
...she changed her mind
about to invite me upstairs for coffee
...on the verge of a glorious sneeze
and it vanished
...I discovered a nice beer
and they discontinued it
...reading the chapter on reproduction
and the school bell rang
...I began to appreciate
a stand-up comic
and he disappeared behind the
veil of sexual misconduct
...I made an interesting friend
and he announced himself
to be a teetotaler
I lost my Nissim Ezekiel in Istanbul
I was on the edge of discovery
That bit where he talks about
writing good poetry.

Sudeep Sen

HAIKU TRIPTYCH
for Nissim Ezekiel

Handwriting
linked-haiku tercets

fingers hold the pen
firmly, guiding the gold nib
in wild cursive scripts —

lines delicately
etched, perfectly pitched with the
stylised slant of a

fine and practised hand —
letterforms and words
bloom, come alive — spell.

*

Fountain Pen

tactile pleasure of
a nib slowly caressing
the skin of a page

*

Writing
phrases, words commune —
elliptical — moulding raw
imagination

Sujatha Mathai

I first met Nissim E. sometime in the 70s, though I'm not absolutely sure. I had been living in small-town Mangalore, after I came back from England. I found myself lonely, unhappy, and adrift. I didn't even know that people were writing poetry in English! After another stint in England (Liverpool), my (former) husband, got a suitable teaching plus surgery post in Bangalore. At last, I could join a theatre group again! I hardly thought about writing, though my very first poem had been accepted by P. Lal. When we moved to Bangalore, I started sending a few poems to *The Indian P.E.N.* journal, edited by Nissim Ezekiel. He was very generous in accepting them, and making me feel I was, maybe? – a poet? After all the misery and isolation I had felt in Mangalore, my life was enriched. About this time, my father, a Professor of English, wrote that he had been invited to a poetry seminar in Jaipur. Would I like to come? We would stay with his very dear, old friend P.S. Sundaram. I agreed. It was there that I first met Nissim Ezekiel! He seemed very friendly and easy to talk to, not highbrow or pretentious as some of the poets seemed to me. He remembered the poems I'd been sending him, and asked me to read a couple of them, including 'In the Market Place', which first appeared in to *The Indian P.E.N.* journal. Later, I was invited to join in a discussion with Nissim on AIR. I don't remember what it was about. But I do remember Nissim's dry sense of humor, which I liked. He was always very kind to me.

Later I started writing more and decided to visit Bombay, where I have many aunts and cousins. I would always make an appointment to meet Nissim. What I noticed about him was his commitment to his work. He worked regularly at the PEN Office, always there, and available to writers and editors who wished to meet him. The dry humor was endearing, as were the postcards, with a few lines on them, signed Nissim E. One day I remember his inviting me for coffee at the Jahangir Art Centre (not sure if that was it), (or was it Samovar?) and we had a lovely chat about literature and people and books. Some people did say rather nasty things about him, but I went by my own experience. Later, he visited Bangalore, and I invited him to tea at my Cunningham Rd house. I was in the throes of an unpleasant break-up, but tried to stay composed. We went once to see him or drop him to the Guest House he was staying at.

I remember my little son saying to Nissim "Can this car fly like a chariot through the crowd?" Nissim said he thought it could!

Nissim was very generous to me. He gave sound criticism, but always used my poems where he could. I'll never forget the thrill and shock I got to find a short poem of mine with a black and white drawing. (I think the poem was called 'The Journey') on the front page of *The Times of India*, edited by Nissim.

Once he gave me a lovely bit of editorial wisdom. I had a line – "held together by sacred bonds". He suggested I change the word "sacred" to "secret". I immediately accepted it as "just right." It was the most innately apt editorial advice I ever received.

He solidly supported my book *The Attic of Night*. I still have the PC on which he wrote: "I believe that your book will go into the third and fourth and more editions."

The Attic of Night sold a thousand copies in its first print, went into a second print, and actually brought me some royalty!

Nissim was on the Board of our Poetry Society of India. The last time I met him was at the Governing Body meeting of the Poetry Society. He seemed ill and disconnected and could not respond to my questions. It was the beginning of his illness, and I hoped he would get the care he needed. I never saw him again.

I am so glad to have his Collected Poems. I think 'The Night of the Scorpion' has become his best known poem. I love many other of his poems, especially 'Background, Casually'.

THE DADDY POEMS

Poems for and about Father

How because you called me
The apple of your eye
Apples will always be special to me.

(from 'Tribute to a Master Poet')

All poems in this section are by Kavita Ezekiel Mendonca

Tribute to a Master Poet
(Inspired by Nissim Ezekiel's poem 'For William Carlos Williams')

I want to write poems like yours

But still, I do not want to
Knowing I cannot, humility is
A sweet pill to swallow.

Everything comes through your poetry
I hear the crescendos
Sudden epiphanies
The cries of your soul
Struggling,
Searching for the light
Defying life
To find meaning in it
Poetic paradoxes you accepted.

I feel the pulse
Of your life's rhythm
In every poem,
Soft and tender
Your hands that write,
They rock me, like they did
The cradle at my birth.

Often, when I read your poems out loud
To myself
Our voices become one
Indistinguishable, blended
In unison we write different lines,
I love duets in music, poetry and dance
A melody of harmony is born

I dreamt of being a back-up singer
For your songs.

Dictate to me
From your heavenly abode
What you would have me say
And I will say it
Verbatim

No complex thought or allusions
Please
Or I will be lost.

If you want to rearrange my words
Check with me first
Be the gentle Father
Then the constructive critic.

Remember how many times
You said you named me
Prophetically
You said I would feel
A stirring in my bones.
That day has come.
My bones have shifted position
Significantly
They are making music.

If, according to you, the prophecy
Has been fulfilled,
Twinkle those eyes
Of approval.
I will continue to write,
With you to thank first
And then the muse.

I am not able to end the poem
Without talking of apples.
It may be a common fruit
How because you called me
The apple of your eye
Apples will always be special to me.

(published in *Sahitya Akademi,* a journal of Indian literature in English, edited by A. J. Thomas, July/August 2020; republished in *Best Asian Poetry,* edited by Sudeep Sen, February 2022)

The Many Things My Father Loved

My father loved the sun
I think the sun loved him back
Unrequited love from the sun
Would be a hard thing for him to bear
After all he had no complaints
About the hot Bombay sun
He wrote poems about it
Loved the sun and the city.

My father loved the moon
Its reflection shone in his eyes
He saw no man or rabbit in it
Only poetry, lines of poems
Floating in the moonlight for him to catch
Transport them to his earthly pages
Paint them with the artist's touch.

My father loved the stars
There was a surge in the twinkle in his eyes
Like a gently rising ocean tide
When he spoke of the stars,
Shooting stars were his favorite
His gravestone told of shooting stars
Across the sky, and how they were a sight to behold
He didn't want to 'burn up, but be seen,'
'That would make sense to him,'
His poem on the gravestone said.

My father loved the sea breeze
He wanted to be buried in the garden
In our home by the sea
So he could feel the breeze on him

Under the earth,
He would be thankful for the coolness.

Above all, my father loved us, his children
Celebrated us in verse and in rhyme
Named me prophetically
So I could write about him
And the many things he loved
It's my turn now, returning in full circle
To declare the things he loved
As I too love the many things he loved
Because it is he who taught me to love them.

(Published in Muse India, edited by Ambika Ananth, May/June 2020)

The Poet's Breath

Walk gently here, careful how and where you step
For here, where girls discarded like candy wrappers,
Where female foetuses destroyed in the still of night
Wrapped in ragged shawls or torn scarves
are left to be devoured by wild animals
in the jungle of survival,
or drowned in rivers
not fortunate enough to be rescued
Like Moses in the bulrushes,
I am she who born free
in the land of the free
Speaks for them.

In that same country, in a hospital
'New Hospital for Women,'
I opened my eyes to my first cry
as a 'new woman.'
Later I would rename the hospital
'Hospital for New Women.'
My mother became a 'new woman'
Changed by my birth.

A poet with a different philosophy
Entered the room
Listened to my first breaths
Cradled me in his arms
Breathed a name on me
Speaking it quietly, almost a whisper
Yet, loud enough for all to hear.
Mother was deaf to my cries,
She had hemorrhaged badly,
Father rejoiced at the birth

Of a girl, his girl
A daughter, born in the land of the free.

He believed his daughter was a gift from his God
She would be named *Kavita, symbolically.
His joy would shower poems on her
While others with girl-children
Knit their brows, puzzled.
Is he crazy, a little touched in the head?
Maybe his poetry made a fool out of him.
What shall I protest?
A girl wanted in a country
Where girls are unwanted?
He wanted me, and took me home
A girl, his daughter, his first-born.

Indian sweets were distributed
Neighbors raised their eyebrows
Surprised, but with silent voices.
'Light-skinned, and hair of golden curls
At least she will not have much trouble
Finding a marriage partner,' they said
'We'll have to check her height and cooking skills,'

My darker skinned friends taunted and teased
While Michael Jackson later sang
"It don't matter if you're black or white."

My aunts and grandmothers simply prayed
I would be like Ruth and like Esther.

May all fathers be poets.
And all aunts and grandmothers pray prayers
For their girls to be women of faith and character

Loved for their hearts and minds
Not their colour.

I want to go home
to this way of life
This kind of land

Kavita is Hindi for poem

(Published in *The Kali Project* edited by Candice Louisa Daquin
and Megha Sood, 2021)

Give me Oil in my Lamp

Grandmother took me to the old synagogue
Walking down the pot-holed sidewalks
of a noisy Bombay street, close to her home,
Every square inch populated with humanity.

The oil lamp in the very old synagogue
hung high from the ceiling
for a few rupees we could keep the light burning.

She was afraid to climb the ladder
provided by the caretaker
in case she missed a step,
I was afraid for her too.
So he took the donation and lit the lamp.
I must cover my head with a handkerchief
she would pray to the prophet Elijah
for the oil never to run out,
The lamp must never die out.

Wanting to know in whose name he could make the receipt
(I did not have a Jewish name)
'Change it for the receipt', she said, matter of factly
'Or the caretaker will get confused'.
So I went from being called *Kavita* to *Elizabeth*
for the sake of a two rupee receipt
I really did not want, or need.
(Mother did want to name me Elizabeth, I recall).

"It's ok. When you get home
You can go back to your real name
Or your father will be upset", grandmother said calmly.

published in *Verse-Virtual*, ed Jim Lewis, June 2021; and in Kavita Ezekiel Mendonca's chapbook *Light of The Sabbath*, 2021.

Those Bombay Sundays

(Inspired by Robert Hayden's poem, 'Those Winter Sundays.')

Those Bombay Sundays
My father woke up his usual 'early'.
'Seize the day', he would say.
He gave the *Carpe Diem* call
on other days too.
Oh, that rising reluctance
on those Bombay Sundays,
Resisting his poetic exhortations.
The crows and pigeons followed the rhythm
of early rising, no matter the day of the week.
Did he want me to turn into a bird?

Then the Black and White TV arrived,
A loan from the National newspaper,
Brought the entire neighborhood with it,
Mostly children, and all those related to them.
Grandmothers needed a helping hand,
to climb the old creaking, wooden staircase
But come, they must, to watch the Sunday Bollywood movie.

Father watched the six o' clock movie,
to write his TV column,
The children sat on the stone floor,
like groundlings at a Shakespeare play,
My aunt sat on the large bed, watching intently
with a grandmother or two,
Begged the husband not to beat his wife,
'It's wrong,' she would say in Marathi.
Calling out the villain to repent of his evil deeds,
Smiling widely when the hero chased the heroine
around the tree, singing romantic songs.

Shifting her weight to the edge of the bed,
when the tension was palpable.
Father wanted to know why the female singers had such high voices.

He had a bemused look on his face
throughout, and with steady stoicism
watched all three hours of the movie,
Took notes on a lined note pad,
Smiled at the children from time to time.

During the intermission
the children stood up, dusted themselves,
Quickly sat down again to watch.

In true Shakespearean groundling style
they called out different 'endings'
to scenes, each according to their tastes.

Those Bombay Sundays
Of the Black and White TV,
When loneliness was unknown,
and no silent snow was falling.

I hear the voices of the children
"Thank you, Uncle, thank you, Uncle,
See you next Sunday."
Daddy loved the children,
kept a few handkerchiefs ready,
for the ones with the runny noses.

"Please come again", he responded to their thanks,
A true Indian-English phrase!
When I say it here, I see the surprise
on the faces of my visitors

I have to explain, it means
they are welcome to visit again
We say it in India, even when exasperated
by some in the constant stream
Of visitors!

Published in *The Usawa Literary Journal*, Issue 5, June 2021; republished in *The Quiver Review*, ed Inam Hussain Begg Mullik, May 2021; included in the *Yearbook of Indian Poetry in English* edited by Vinita Agrawal and Sukrita Paul Kumar, June 2021.

Bombay Monsoon

A box of old photographs
becomes a magician with his tricks
Pulls me out of his hat as a little girl
My hair in two pony tails
The greyness of age covered in curls of gold and brown.

Time places me on the stone steps
of the small rented family home
in pouring rain, listening for the deep-throated croaking
of the frogs, audible but camouflaged
behind the dripping bushes of the lush garden.
My ears fill with the laughter of the street urchins
splashing, pushing cars in the flooded waters
smiling gratitude for a few coins to buy peanuts,
bananas, or any kind of cheap food.
The smell of fresh earth invades the nostrils
the voice of father calling out
'Come inside, you'll get wet.'

I am chasing my paper boat
already sailed away to a distant shore
My hands too small to reach it.
The Bombay rain is heaven opened
God has inundated the earth with his bounty.
I am standing in the pouring rain
No grey in my rain-drenched hair

I leave the box of old photographs open,
The little girl lives inside me and in the box
Only the rain feels a little different here
I long for the rain with the frogs, urchins and paper boats.
On this distant shore where I am placed
And must call home, albeit by own choice

My one complaint, about the rain
We don't use the word 'monsoon' here.
We call it 'wet weather.'
'Monsoon' sounds more romantic!

(published in *Verse-Virtual*, ed Jim Lewis, February 2022)

Bombay Fish Market

Here the entire sea
Comes in with the fish
Wet, Wet, Wet,
Everything is wet
The stench, indescribable!
Bell-bottoms and flipflops
Not appropriate apparel
In a Bombay fish market.
Mother scolds me for making
Poor dress choices.

The fisherwomen loaded with gold ornaments
Jasmine flowers in their hair
Call out in raucous voices,
The fish wear sad expressions
Lying on stone slabs
in salt sea-water.

Mother bargains with her usual style
The fisherwoman says
"I'll sell you the fish cheap
if you give your daughter's hand in marriage to my son".
That was the last time
I went to the fish market with mother.
Fish curry at home erases
The fish market experience.
Still the enjoyment of the curry
Comes tinged with a bit of guilt
Sadness for the fish
on the stone slabs, their eyes follow me.

Father takes me to the Aquarium
A once-in-a-while treat.
A better place to admire fish.
Still my preference is to go down to the sea with him
Where I dream of writing a poem
like John Masefield's *Sea Fever.*
The fish are at home in the ocean
That travels the shores of my city.
I wish for everything Masefield desires
Unlike him, I am afraid of the sea.

(published in *Verse-Virtual*, ed Jim Lewis, August 2021; republished in Silver Birch Press's *One Good Memory* series, October 2022)

This is the City
(After the nursery rhyme, 'This is the House that Jack Built.')

This is the city my father loved
That he called home, that wrote his poems,
That created the slums, that built the skyscrapers
That jammed the trains, that crowded the buses
Where he walked the streets – that somebody built.

This is the city that I have loved
Where I was born where I was raised
Where I ran for the buses, in four-inch heels
Danced in discos all night long, studied in the colleges,
          sang in choirs
Dated the boys, then married a man – that I loved.

This is the city where I lived by the sea
Ate street food, shopped fiercely, listened to Rock music
Read Enid Blyton, Barbara Cartland, Ayn Rand,
          borrowed from friends,
Practiced for Sports Day, studied for exams – that I did not love.

This is the city that I have left, I know not why, I cannot remember
This is the city lodged in my soul, something stuck in a tooth,
          I cannot remove.
This is the city that I still love, with its dust and grime,
          will always be mine
That I must in Hindi call *'Bombay Meri Jaan'*,
          meaning Bombay my love
A city whose name I no longer can pronounce –
          a city that is now called Mumbai.

(published in *Verse-Virtual* August 2021; and included in the anthology *Around The World Landscapes and Cityscapes, edited by Steve Carr,* Sweetycat Press, 2021)

Sixth Floor

Mother was the last flower
plucked from the garden
of our ground floor flat.
Transplanted to the sixth floor
of a seven-storey building,
She could no longer see the stars
or smell the sea and hear the waves,
Sitting on the chairs with father and the children
Late into the night
under the heavens.

In a place not of her choosing,
her roots didn't take hold.
The building sat at the top
of a steep slope.
Her flower, though watered frequently,
Began to wilt on the sixth floor,
Trapped in a jungle of concrete.
There were more flowers like her,
Fading in the buildings,
she could see from the windows.
Little consolation.

Where once she had walked
With the cool grass beneath her feet,
Now, she held onto a chair.
Lifted one knee up to touch her waist,
then put it down.
Lifted the next knee up, then down,
'I've done my exercise', she said.
The elephants in the Yamini Roy painting
That hung above the dining table
seemed to wear a puzzled look!

Father offered a solution,
as he always did.
'I'll hold your hand tightly
Up and down the slope.
We'll walk to the sea,
It will still be the same.
It hasn't moved, like us,
We'll go after dinner
The stars will be out.'

Mother wanted to go back
To the garden
To be a flower in that flower bed,
She promised to bloom
as she had once done
Where the soil was fertile
for her dreams.
When she talked about it
The sixth floor wore
an air of nostalgia
and smelled of the sea.
I looked out at the sky
I thought I saw
The same twinkling stars.

The elephants in the Yamini Roy painting
that hung above the dining table
returned to their original expression.
They looked serene, just like before
When the painting hung above the red curtain
in our ground floor flat.
seemed to know she was talking about
Their first home, hers, mine, ours

They had watched her
Sitting in the garden
Smelling the sea, gazing at the stars.
Not aging and with no knee problems.
They lifted their trunks slightly
Perhaps they smelled the perfume of flowers
Filling the air.
The garden was her healer
The elephants knew the secret.

(published in *The Quiver Review*, ed Inam Hussain Begg Mullik, May 2021)

sans punctuation
a prose poem

when i was ten i started writing poetry and showed it to my father who was a poet and he asked me where the punctuation was and why i was writing poems without commas or full stops or other punctuation so as i am writing a lot of poetry these days i am constantly thinking of father but more about his words so as a kind of tribute to him and since i write many poems about him and dedicated to him i have written a satiric poem on what a poem looks like without punctuation so this poem is meant to be purposefully read in one breath since it has no punctuation which if there were commas and full stops it would mean stopping to breathe and pausing at different points since punctuation is like normal breathing and since poetry is a mirror of life and life is the breath of poetry then if i added the punctuation you would have to pause to take a breath so now i must stop for fear of causing discomfort or death for to stop breathing is the essence of the certainty of dying and i do not want to be responsible for a reader's death metaphorically speaking and now in a little while after the next few lines you may please breathe although there is no full stop at the end of the poem and you just have to trust the poet's word and breathe i just wanted to add that i was good at grammar in school having had an excellent foundation with wren and martin the bible of grammar just so the reader is aware that i know exactly where this prose poem needs punctuation and i really want to thank my readers for bearing with me and reading a different kind of poem so thank you and i do hope that not capitalising the uncapitalized has reminded some of you of the way the poet e e cummings often signed his name and i hope that i have finally my father happy now that i am quite conscious of using proper punctuation when I write my poetry
(published in the *RIC Journal* (Red In Corner journal Jaipur), ed Saudamini Deo, December 2021)

How Daddy wrote his Poetry

Between puffs of a Menthol Cool cigarette
left to curl In the glass ashtray
the folded handkerchief carefully placed on eyes
He lay in silent wait for the Muse
to bring him the lines.

The delicately-crafted glasses
set aside on the untidy desk
the faithful typewriter in the centre
the cheques he had forgotten to deposit
becoming bookmarks of a different kind
the turtle shaped coin box for 'loose change'
were all part of a familiar scene.

There was a pattern to the rhythm
as he moved from bed to desk
Writing words and lines
on pieces of paper, blank or lined
whatever could be found
Then back to the bed again.

He breathed deeply.
Or deep 'breathely',
as he was fond of saying,
Perhaps invoking the muse
for the rest of the poem
to take shape.
Breathing gave pause to the poetic process.

Pacing up and down the sparsely furnished room
Reading the words aloud
inviting me in

to be both audience and critic
Completed the ceremony.

Daddy typed with two fingers
on the old clickety typewriter
The manuscript was ready
to be delivered to willing eyes.

Daddy wrote often
Into the early hours of the morning
And I had to creep into the room
Mouse-like
Cockroach quiet,
Remove the handkerchief
Turn off the light
I tell him
He must sleep.
It's late, Daddy!

I stood outside his room
until I heard the familiar click
of the old wooden latch
and I knew he'd get a few hours
Of fulfilled slumber.

(Published in *Verse-Virtual*, ed Jim Lewis, June 2022)

Family Sunday

Unsummoned, we assemble
And slowly go
To the same place
At the same time
As though destiny decrees it.
We sit on the same stones
Provided by the beach,
Sea and sky
Reflected in our eyes.
We make the same remarks
In praise of what we see,
Only the lovers
Excluded from the scene
Respectably.

To eat something
Is part of the ceremony,
So we eat.
To leave when it is dark
Is part of the ceremony,
So we leave
When it is dark.

We call it a Family Reunion
My father makes his Sunday joke
About Eliot's play
My mother laughs, alone.
They both agree
that this is the way
to spend a happy Sunday evening.
We children
Are supposed to be content
And not want a change.

(From *Family Sunday and Other Poems* by Kavita Ezekiel, first published by Peacock Publishers, Bombay, January 1989; second edition: October 1990)

Loss

Dedicated to my father
who sadly passed away from Alzheimer's in 2004

My father could not talk to me
Before he died
Could not reach me in a distant land
Twinned in spirit, separated by geography,
I heard he remembered me
Said he could never forget me
Memory without a memory
Not able to remember
Not able to forget
Trapped in a maze of loss.
Two losses
The greater loss is mine

Thankfully,

He could not remember
What he had lost.

(Published in the online portal, *Poetry India, ed Udayan Thakkar*)

Mother

On the August day that I was born
It was a glorious Bombay morn
Mother said she almost died
No one heard me when I cried
No one cared about the baby
Would she survive? the verdict was maybe
The doctors they all rushed about
While I continued to scream and shout
The doctors worked hard to save a life
To give me a mother, and a husband his wife,
Then father entered the hospital room
Didn't understand the darkness and gloom
Held me tightly in his loving arms
Twinkled his eyes and turned on his charms
Named me his 'poem' and thanked his wife
She had given him the gift of a new life
Glad that I had a head of curls
But more than glad that I was a girl!
Today I remember my mother with pride
In giving me life she almost died.
It's never easy to lose a mother
For she is a woman like none other.
When the daisies bloom in summer
Every flower has the face of my mother.

*The word "poem" refers to my name, Kavita, which means poem
in Hindi.

To Carry the Torch
A poem dedicated to preserving the legacy of my father.

To carry the torch
Fingers must first learn
To hold the lighted matchstick
Right to the very end
Feel the heat of the burning wood
Before relinquishing it to the ground.
Have no fear
Of the lighted matchstick
The secret is practice.

To carry the torch
Speak a blessing on the hands
That passed it on to you
The one gone before
That ignited the flame
Speak your gratitude to your stars.

To carry a torch
Legs must train
Till pain fills the body
Increase the threshold of pain
Run up the steps to the very top.

Carry the torch to light the flame
Keep it burning
Let nothing extinguish it.

How Many Issues Do You Have?
Very Indian Tale in Very Indian English: Based on a true story

In India also
Gujaratis, Maharashtrians, Hindiwallahs
All brothers –
Though some are having funny habits.
Still, you tolerate me,
I tolerate you,
– 'The Patriot' by Nissim Ezekiel

Father is never remembering names of people
All of us are knowing that.
Sometimes that is causing
So much confusion.

One hot sweaty Bombay afternoon
Man was sweating, Father was sweating.
Man was walking beside him
From Bombay Central station
All the way to the house
Where father lived,
Asking and asking about each member of his parent's family
By name,
"How is this one?"
"How is that one?"
He was not stopping his questions
He was following and following.

Father kept shaking his head
From side to side
As Indians are wont to do.
"Fine," he said.
"Everyone is fine,"

Father was having much *fedupness*.
Finally, the man asked
"And how many issues do you have?"

Now issues in *Olde* English
Means children
And that's what the man meant,
In those days
My father had brought out a magazine
Called 'Poetry India'
He thought the man was asking
About that.
So he replied
''I have one issue coming out
Every month."

The man was turning purple with surprise
''How that is possible?"
"Nobody can be doing that."
The man was still asking.
"Easy," said father
"You just have to work hard
To bring it out, if you love
What you do."
"You are very prolific,"
Man was still commenting
Now in completely bewildered state.
Tipping his *topi to father
Man briskly retraced his steps
To the Bombay Central Station
catching the first train back home
Telling his wife, 'these poets
Are very different kind of people!'

Father reached home
And narrated the story to me
"Indians are such strange people,"
He said,
we must be strange too
Since we are also Indians!
And who was that person, anyway?
But he was still not remembering.

Simply Father was misunderstanding
That issues was having many meanings.
Pun was hiding and escaping
But still we were laughing
At ourselves.
And that is nice thing to do.

Topi is an Indian word for hat

Waiting for Daddy

Daddy, the poets have gone home now
They have taken their commas and full stops with them
You must be hungry now, daddy
Let's have lunch together,
I have brought along my poem
But it can wait,
I can wait.
Eat slowly, take your time, enjoy your meal
Let's laugh together
At those silly 'knock knock' jokes
You love to tell,
Don't worry about the clever student
Who will be waiting in the wings
To ask you questions about your life
And then ask others, who with masks of love
Rob a man of his private suffering
To indulge a world with its love of sensationalism.

You answer the questions about your poetry
You authorize

You are not public property anymore, daddy
Private Property, no trespassing.

You took your answers to the grave
We were splashed with the mud
And they with false fame,
How little it mattered to them,
They who chose ignorance
Of how we waited for you
With our poems and our love
And how it broke our hearts…

(Published in *Explorations in English Poetry*, edited by Jaydeep
Sarangi, 2021)

Mother

Mother had three sarees
Two were 'inside sarees' to wear in the house
The third was the 'going out' saree to wear for occasions,
She could wear the 'inside' one to the bazaar
Which was outside the house,
So that was the "inside-outside" saree.

Mother fried onions at four-thirty in the morning.
When they became too expensive, we rejoiced
She made the curry without onions,
Then there was no smell and our sleep was blissful.
At five-thirty she packed 'hot lunch'
Into lunch boxes.
With no microwaves we ate our 'hot lunch' cold,
With few ingredients and a limited budget
Mother's food was heavenly.
She took cooking lessons from Premila Lal.

In mother's world you had to eat the egg soft-boiled
Or egg-flip, if you had sports practice
At six-thirty in the morning,
Egg-flip was raw egg in warm milk
No nutmeg. Condiments are expensive
Only for the rich.
Close your nose and drink it up, or down.
If you didn't, she would hold your nose
For you and you couldn't breathe.

Mother had an idiom for everything,
Some she recited in English, others in Marathi
If you failed a math test, it was
'Don't cry over spilt milk,'

She said my daddy was 'too clever by half'*
        (sounded better in Marathi)
If he rationalized matters by 'clever' intellectual arguments,
Remember he was a poet!
One day she took me to see the Principal of her old school
Who asked how my daddy was
My reply, 'my daddy is too clever by half.'
Mother did not flinch when the Principal asked
Where I had learned that expression.

Mother rolled her eyes to communicate commands
She rolled one lip over the other, pressing them hard together
It was a language learned in childhood
A call to prompt response as children.

Once I tried to express disapproval of a student's behaviour
I rolled my eyes and pressed my lips together hard
He burst out laughing, I failed to understand his response
Mother's face appeared before me
More practice might be needed.

Many things in the world according to my mother
Make so much sense to me now.
The ritual of hand-washing, great for Pandemic times,
Between fingers, in, out, over palms under hands
Her legacy of 'Waste not, Want not'
'Saving for a Rainy Day'
And her prophecy for my future
"The world will become a more difficult place for you
And even more difficult for your children
But remember that God is great."
I'm glad I inherited her faith.

*'Too clever by half' in idiomatic usage refers to being too clever for your own good.

(published in the anthology, *Poetry—The Best of 2020,* Inner Child Press International)

My Father's Eyes

I see the stars in my Father's eyes
He shared his truths, and he was wise
I know the waves in father's hair
I hear his footsteps on the stair
I feel the poems which flowed from his hands
Some were spontaneous, some were planned
I sense his spirit of fun and laughter
In good measure, he left some to his daughter
I touch his words upon the page
He was the same on and off stage
More alive to me than you may think
Visit sometime and together
Let's have a small drink
Footprints on the sands of time
Walk on, rock on, daddy
I'm following right behind
But wait
Two sets of footprints side by side
Flowing together like a gentle tide.

The Black Bicycle
(After William Carlos Williams…only longer)
For father, who taught me how to ride my first bicycle.

So much depends
On a black bicycle
Resting serenely against
The overflowing petunias in the window boxes
And the rain drenched cushions
On the patio.
The cushions are sun- dried now
The cherry tomatoes will soon be red.

I may lie down on the patio
With a handkerchief over my eyes
Like my poet father did on his bed,
Waiting for words,
Dreaming of lines like his.

In the garden of my childhood
I sense his hands holding the bicycle
Then the letting go
As I fell, many times.
Death took over, as it must do
The permanence of the letting go.

Now, I fall many times,
While I watch the purple pansies
With their faces upturned
To meet the sun.
I no longer ride bicycles.
Without father,
The balance is difficult,
Yet, the poems of childhood

Drift in and out in solid shapes
Sometimes, I sense his invisible hands
Guiding my words and lines.

(published in *Verse-Virtual*, ed Jim Lewis, June 2022)

When Poets Pass
In loving memory of my father, the late poet Nissim Ezekiel

When poets pass beyond the world of poetry
To that other world of promised greater beauty
Where lines will be written on stars
Sent shooting in shafts of light to earth,
Flags must fly half-mast, heads must bow.

My poet father gone too early, I learned in a phone call
The old typewriter mourned in silence
The purple ribbon faded and sad,
He gave me life, seeds to plant my garden
My blood, the colors of his Poetry.

The poet lives in veins and arteries of my body
I am named to carry the legacy
Breathing life into me through poems and postcards.
I was not there to throw a handful of earth
On his lowered grave, my father,
The reluctant earth gave back the words
I would have choked to speak then
Now, in this eulogy
I might be able to say a few words.

Meanwhile we must continue to mourn and weep
The poet's journey has been long and steep
Turning night to day and day to night
Writing to redeem the world's plight,
His road continues beyond the grave
Gifting words and precious memories to save
He labours at his desk while the moon is out
While I am left to dream and doubt
The mysteries of life and death
Feeling his absence with every breath.

Night of the Snake
Tandem poem to Nissim Ezekiel's poem 'Night of the Scorpion'
And for my son, Siddharth (Sid), so he would know what
transpired that night.

It was not Lawrence's snake
Waiting patiently for me at the water trough
But a different snake camouflaged
on the stone wall outside our home
in the gently rolling hills
across the gleaming lake
The night dark with the pouring rain
Fear was a knot in my heart.

He seemed to have a right to be there
To be at home
His name on the nameplate,
I address him as 'he', unable to distinguish
A male snake from a female one.

The innocent child asleep in my arms
Knew nothing of the danger
Posed to him by the creature
Resting like a still-life painting
Etched in curves of slithery colors
An artist's rendering of beauty and evil
Simultaneously.

It did not move or
Rear its head to
Hiss or spit poisonous venom
at the sleeping child,
Wet from his soaking clothes.

My other companion
Began to dance madly
A Rumpelstiltskin of fear,
While frantic to appease the curled one
Begged her to remain still
Simply to utter a silent prayer
To whatever God she believed in.

Unaware, the child's father
Watched a movie with the school children
In the hall above,
Unsuspecting of the drama unfolding below.

I turned the key in the lock
The house door silently opened
Granting safe entry to mother and child,
My companion having fled to safer terrain
Leaving the snake at repose, immovable.
No neighbors to help or witness the spectacle
No peasants to chant their incantations
To pray the snake would return
to its snake home.

Creeping outside once more
With beating heart and stealthy pace,
to narrate the tale to the child's father
The sleeping child, now dry,
Oblivious to the imminent danger
From the curled serpent on the stone wall
He had gone from whence he came
Into the dark recesses of his own mind,
Curled on someone else's door perhaps,
Or waiting silently for an unsuspecting prey-moment
No creature or human understanding could comprehend.

Thank goodness for Divine intervention
That granted protection to the precious child.
I wrapped the bundle tighter,
Afraid it might still be watching me,
From somewhere.

Note: Tandem poetry is a genre I have created for poems I write alongside my father's poems. The subjects may be similar since they are inspired by him, but the content of the poems is mine.

Wildness

I love a little wildness.
To speak more truth, I love it a lot.

Flowers growing jungle-like
Minus the tigers and lions of wild India,
Wild horses on the Alberta prairies
Tossing freely their flowing manes
Wild owls even if they are garden statues
A wild restless mind roaming my unmowed lawn.
A garden with dandelions despite treatment from 'Weedman'
Our faithful service provider who fertilizes and aerates the lawn
Eradicator of wild mushrooms and dandelions.

I write poetry under a wildly hot summer sun
Celebrating wildness with a little sunscreen
The swing cover has blown off many summers ago
I reject the neat colorful umbrellas
I have two in the garage
I will have to leave them as legacy
For the children, not wild, yet not quite tamed!

At night, the shape of a lone coyote
Is silhouetted in the distance
We watch from the car
On our drive through the park
He roams wild and free.
The foxes can be heard
From the open bedroom windows
From their barks, seems they take comfort in numbers
Barking wildly unmindful of human sleep
Two Bobcats cry like children
My compassionate father would have gone out

In the dead of night to stop them
'They might get hurt', he would have said
I hear him, but my fear of bobcats and the night
Drown out all thoughts of compassion.

Wildness and imperfection are travelling companions
Hand-in hand like a honeymooning couple.
Father would have said
'A little imperfection improves the taste of life'.
We played madly in the mud back home
The dust blew into the meal on the table
In Bombay dust is part of the psyche
'A little dust improves the taste of the food'
Father often said with that twinkle in his eyes.

Mother protests 'this is not an English proverb'
Who can argue with her?
She has a degree in English.

We grew up on sayings about spicing up our lives
With dust and imperfection
with wildness of the poetic kind
Otherwise known as imagination.

If there is a wild child in every family
And I am the chosen one
I ask that I be allowed to wear that mantle
With grace.

Haibun of the Able Seaman

It is incredible what a man will do when he wants to return to his home in India, from a foreign land, where his companions for three years had been philosophy, poetry and poverty, his lodging an 'attic with mice for friends', that's how he described it to me. Perhaps that was a metaphor; his way of explaining cheap accommodation. My inclination is as always, to believe him. What irony to learn that this same man would win an award for being a deck hand! It's a true story I never tire of hearing about… certificate of 'Able Seaman' awarded to him, my poet father. A father with a slender fame, delicate glasses that would blow into the waves of the ocean, at the hint of the faintest breeze, and the thin wrists that made him always want to wear a long-sleeved shirt, to cover them. By the longest stretch of my imagination, I can't picture him scrubbing the decks of the cargo ship, carrying coal to Indochina. His companion, who was supposed to travel with him would later change his mind, so he would travel alone. He braved the elements with that same determination that kept him abroad for four long years. Despite the 'three P's', his constant companions, (the philosophy and poetry, he didn't mind) the call of home becoming stronger than ever, he must find a way to return. Perhaps the sea had a poetry of its own, made its own music, in the sound of the wind on the waters. His ocean journey would land him in his beloved city, Bombay, to carve words into posterity.

Nothing seemed to relieve the tedium of the life of a deckhand on board, engaged in the most menial of tasks. It would seem that nature or fate conceals her rewards, however small or insignificant to others, and reveals them at the opportune moment. The aspiring poet was delighted when Fortune Press in London, agreed to publish his book for a certain sum of money. Of course he didn't have it, when a friend came to the rescue, and the money was duly paid.

What are the chances that after sailing from London, he would be pleasantly surprised with copies of his first book of poems waiting for him in Marseilles, at the forwarding address he had provided? He could never have imagined this turn of events. The poet's real journey had begun.

Call of the homeland
Poems in wind, waves, water
The human spirit

(published in *SETU Magazine*, 'Voices Within' Special Poetry section, ed Gopal Lahiri, 2020)

The Poet's Desk Haibun

It was one of those old wooden desks he probably inherited from his father, who being a "Science" man, could never have imagined his son a poet. Through the passing of so many years, I can still feel the grain of the desk, smell the wood, touch the paper, and breathe the dust. I can visualize all of it, from my writing desk in a different country. The man, silhouetted now, behind the old desk is my father. I see him clearly – bespectacled, sitting calmly behind all that clutter. Repeated offers to clean and organize all the poems, written on lined and plain paper, that lay and floated in random piles everywhere, were declined. I suppose there was 'a method in his madness.' The old manual typewriter that sat resolutely in the middle, surrounded by dusty but meaningful creativity, cried out for a change of ribbon from time to time. There were open-paged books too, autographed by poets from every country, where he had been invited to read his poems. For a bookmark, in one of the books he was reading, was an outdated cheque, now long expired! Some passports, new and old showed their faces, peeping out among the papers, a tortoise-shaped coin box for 'loose change,' which my daughter inherited as a gift from him, and some rupee notes between poems. The dust seemed to love his poetry and was permanently settled in generous amounts on words and lines. The light from the window captured the dust particles as if a Fairy Godmother had sprinkled stardust from her magic wand.

His bed, beside his desk, wore a similar appearance, except for the handkerchiefs he used to cover his eyes when he lay down as he waited for the words to come. Sitting here at my desk, which is nothing like his, I wonder why a man is judged by the way he keeps his desk. I heard so many comments about his desk, from fellow writers and others, about the clutter and the dust. It reminds me of the old adage, 'don't judge a book by its cover.'

The feel of old grain
The desk writes its words and lines
Here sat a poet

(published in the online portal, *Indian Periodical, ed Siddharth Sehgal,* April the 2nd, 2023)

At Seventeen

The muezzin from the nearby mosque
calls the faithful to prayer
The church bells across the street ring
The Rabbi chants the Hebrew prayers
with shawl and Kippah, swaying, bending
back and forward, forward and back
in the end-of-lane synagogue.
I stand at the window
in a house full of people
My loneliness, undiagnosed.
The window is green,
that's just the color of the paint
My world has a different color.
They don't put you in a hospital
for loneliness, you must find
your own cure.
The love of a mother perhaps?

I am seventeen and very young,
I want another option to living.

My loneliness has a smell
to my nose only, my clothes wear it.
Glued to the window with elbows.
I am frozen, an ice sculpture,
searching for relief for my solitude,
I am alone, deep inside
where nobody can see.
Plunged into darkness
'The darkness has its
secrets which the light does not know'*

Below, in the streets
the throng of people swarm like buzzing bees,
Unsuspecting of the misery above
Oblivious, blissfully filling the streets.

They all look happy to me, perhaps an illusion
of the happiness I craved
Illusion painted in green.

My mother is a bus ride away
I still don't understand her reasons
for sending me away
She jokes one child was exchanged
in the hospital
at seventeen you cannot take a joke
like that.
I have my father's curls
like waves of the sea
Inherited his 'live and let live' attitude.
Both poetic dreamers, feet firmly planted in the air,
Both. Each, Lonely in our own way.
She is lonely too, my mother.
all things worldly left for her to do,
cooking, banking and long-term planning,
Alone, a different kind of loneliness.

My father says my decision to die
will shatter the family
No family at the window at seventeen,
Alone at the green window.
'Express your grief in a poem,'
He says, 'you will feel better.'
The usual response for my pain,
any kind of pain.

He wrote me a letter,
a letter lost in space.
The panacea for all ills is Poetry,
The world according to father.

I am still alive, not seventeen anymore
With children of my own,
That was a passing phase
A long and dark tunnel
For one so young.

Vulnerability was a raw wound
Hope has a new meaning now.
If I knew then what I know now
I would not have stood at that window
Filled my ears with rock music
Cancelled out the sounds of misery
Rock and Roll Music
Reverberating in brain wave
After brain wave.
Something to dance to
Something to still the grief
Of dying alone
At the green window.

I am still writing poetry
I took father's advice
But the pain is raw
The knife stops its twisting
In random moments of happiness.
I am collecting the pain fragments
To bury when it's time
To die a natural death.

Mother apologises for sending me away
She says it's the only thing she regrets
In her life.
I visit her in the old-age home
Her face is expressionless.
I weep.
'Why are you crying?' she says, 'I did say I'm sorry.'
But *I* was more than sorry
What she didn't know
I was sorry she didn't have a better life.

*quoted from a poem by Nissim Ezekiel
(published in the anthology *Through the Looking Glass*, edited by
Candice Louisa Daquin et al, IndieBlu(e) Publishing May 2021)

My Father taught me Love

I remain in love with Bombay
The city with its old name
Still flows my veins, beats my heart in steady rhythm
The waves of the sea throb my pulse.
My father taught me to love the sea and the city
With its old name.

I stood beside my father's grave
At the old Jewish cemetery across the racecourse
There was his poem about a shooting star
Engraved on it with a Star of David,
I thought I heard him recite the poem
I wept, careful not to erase the lines
His voice mellifluous and poignant
He made me fall in love with poetry.

I visited the old house seventeen years ago
Where I played in the garden as a child
With all the neighborhood children
A tall building had replaced the trees and flowers
I gazed at the changed landscape and reminisced,
I saw my father watching happily as I played
He was standing on the stone steps
His eyes like twinkling stars
My father taught me to love trees.

With broken sandals my father walked the streets
He travelled by the crowded trains
He rubbed shoulders with humanity
He wanted to carve poems on the sidewalks
He taught me to embrace the crowds
He taught me to love the city of my birth
To fall in love with Bombay.

My father taught me to love Thoreau
He said not everyone can go 'to the woods'
One must build a 'cabin' in the city
To learn not to lead a life of 'quiet desperation.'
My father taught me to love the woods, the stars and the city.

(published in the anthology *Soul Spaces*, edited by Swati Pal, Anita Nahal, et. al., 2023)

Of Flaws and Gifts

After Nissim Ezekiel's poem 'I Met a Man Once'

I was born to a man
Who could not drive a car
Typed with two fingers
Never learned to use a computer,
(His critics got him for this one).
Not knowing what he wanted in a clothing store
Needing advice on color, style and type.
Rejoiced when he discovered the secret to boiling an egg
Simply because he thought
there was a secret to it.
Was lost when it came to banking
How many zeros in one thousand, ten thousand?
Where to sign the cheque?
Worldly affairs were beyond him
His feet firmly planted in the air.

I knew this man intimately,
A gentle man, a kind man, a simple man
Eyes that twinkled like stars on a clear night,
Magnanimous with money and time
Faithful mentor to young poets,
Who could not bear to watch a child crying
Or a prostitute being beaten up
Who didn't have many shirts
But would give the shirt off his back
To anyone in need, or not in need.

Yet, he knew how to write a poem
With words that could
Shimmer the moonlight
Make the sun shine brighter

Ripple the water, sparkle the stars
Tell stories that rocked your world with laughter
Praise God for his gifts and admit his failures.

I know that man well
For he was my father
I have his flaws
In my genes
And perhaps a little
From his gift of words.

(published in *Different Truths* online magazine, ed Arindam Roy, January the 9th, 2023)

The Dancing Professor

Seated in the middle row
of the old, University classroom
on hard benches that hurt the body
Surrounded by eager friends
Hungry for the truths of Literature
I watched the bespectacled professor
in his maroon khadi kurta climb on to the dais
(He had blue, ochre, brown khadi kurtas too
In his collection)
Each lecture colored by a different hue.

He was teaching rhythm and meter in poetry
Iambic, trochaic, spondaic, anapestic, dactylic.
From the dais to the front of the class
He began to gallop like a horse
He explained it was called Anapestic rhythm
Also known as the galloping rhythm.

The students applauded
I hung my head and averted his gaze
You see, the professor in the colorful kurta
Was my father!

At home I asked why he galloped in front of the students
He simply said 'Poetry is a dance of words.'

(published in online magazine, *Verse-Virtual*, ed Jim Lewis,
January 2023)

Peace At All Costs
Father's mantra 'Peace at all costs'

Calmed our sibling quarrels
Our petty squabbles soon forgotten
We resumed our play with dolls and toys.

'Peace at all costs, he said to me
Standing beside mother, facing me
as I tried to win an argument with her.
Smiling gently through his fragile glasses
His eyes twinkling like stars.

'Peace at all costs,' he said
To the man beating his wife
During a late night altercation
On the street outside our home.
Father didn't know the local language
So he took me along to translate
'Shanti, Shanti' I repeated
The man looked startled, the wife disappeared into the darkness.

There would be no war if there was 'Shanti.'
Peace begins at home, I learnt as a child.
I asked my father more on the meaning of his mantra
How much do I need to pay for peace?
What is the cost?
'Very little,' he said, 'it's not expensive'
(He was a poet and taught life through metaphors)
His reply showed me the importance of peace
In resting our differences quietly
Letting the earth be one earth
All people be one people
The animals, the heavens, flora and fauna
Bathe in the same sunshine.

In my father's mantra, I find peace.
In all languages peace is peace
Shanti, Paz, Pace, Shalom, Paix

I've sometimes paid the price for peace
The budget expanded to afford it
No spreadsheet tracker needed to keep accounts.

(Published in *Different Truths Magazine*, edited by Arindam Roy,
March, 2023)

The Last Poem
(For my poet father who sadly passed away from Alzheimer's)

In your simple nursing home room
Friends and family placed paper and pen
on the small table beside the bed
Hoping you would do what you loved
So dearly your whole life,
Write one more poem, even if it were your last.

I wasn't there, but from past experience
when you had the cataract operation
and the doctor ordered rest for the eyes
Which of course you did not heed
I imagine you fumbled in your pocket
for your train pass and said your usual:
'I have to catch the 8:15 train to Churchgate station
Or I'll be late to the *P.E.N. office
I am needed there.'

Writing a poem might awaken the brain
Friends and family believed,
I saw you staring vacantly at the ceiling
in the photograph they sent me.

Perhaps if the sun, moon, stars, sky
a few trees and a calming wind
had 'waltzed' into the room
Your poem would take shape
Or perhaps they should move you
To a more inspiring environment.

You have left the earth
The trains from Bombay Central to Churchgate

Come and go, they are more crowded.
Someone else is at the P.E.N. office now
They still talk about you
Your desk piled high with manuscripts
You, surrounded by poets and writers.

Now, I write the poems
to keep your memory alive
I don't have to, it happens naturally,

You are so alive in every poem you wrote
Your 'Collected Works' is my other Bible
Your twinkling eyes brighten my lines
Their spark of mischief enhance the images.

You often said 'I am needed there at the office,'
Do you know how much you are needed here?

One day, I will read my poems to you
My prayer is to be granted the patience
to wait for that day.

*P.E.N. Poets, Editors, Playwrights, Essayists, Novelists, is a world-wide literary organization. My father worked for the one in Bombay, now Mumbai.

(Published in *Madras Courier*, edited by Shrenik Rao, April, *2023*)

Knots

The story started with 'Once upon a time'
Expected to end with 'Happily ever after.'
The Fairy Tales I read as a child
Promised such an ending
Art should imitate life.

Like monkeys in a barred cage
We kept vigil all that dark night
Then fell asleep one by one
Like koalas drunk on eucalyptus leaves
We fell exhausted on the bed.
The stars grew weary, the moon hid behind a cloud
Only she remained awake till morning light
the grass wet with dew, the sun still shy.

He never came home, never returned
The colored glass pieces in the kaleidoscope
No longer made meaningful patterns
I became Humpty Dumpty whom
'All the kings horses and all the kings men'
Could not put back together.

I want to be *Kintsugi*
Lacquer dusted with powdered gold, silver or platinum.
I want to untie the knots in my stomach
Play jump rope as in childhood days.
Before he left
My hair tossing in the wind
Carefree.

I want to be Kintsugi
Broken but fixable

I want the light
To come in through the cracks.

(Due for publication in the forthcoming anthology of South
Asian Women's poetry, *Trauma,* edited by Lopamudra Basu and
Feroza Jussawalla).

INTERVIEWS

Photo credit: Shalva Weil.

Writers in Conversation: Interview with Kavita Ezekiel Mendonca

Basudhara Roy and Jaydeep Sarangi
https://journals.flinders.edu.au/index.php/wic/article/view/76/86
This interview was conducted via emails
in the rainy days of June, 2020.

Q. So, you are a poet, the bearer of a poetic legacy and you are so lyrically called 'Kavita'. Tell us about how poetry happened to you?

I am so pleased you asked this question at the very outset of the interview. Thank you for that. My name Kavita, for which I have my father, the late poet Nissim Ezekiel, to be forever grateful to means 'Poetry' in Hindi. My father was the 'Kavi' (Poet) and I was his 'Kavita'. Shakespeare said, 'A rose by any other name would smell as sweet,' but I wonder sometimes, if I had a different name, would I perhaps have been a different person? Of all the Jewish and Indian names available to him, my father seems to have put some conscious thought to giving me a name which reflected something that was of prime importance to him in life. My mother must have understood this, because she acquiesced too. I never heard mention of any controversy over my name in the home. My grandfather spoke Sanskrit, but I am not sure if that had anything to do with it. He was a "Science man" and didn't really understand my father's passion for poetry, but never objected to it either. He let all his children follow their dreams. In one of my poems, "The Many things my Father loved,' published in the May-June issue of Muse India, I make mention of the significance of my naming. My father...

Named me prophetically
So I could write about him
And the many things he loved

It's my turn now, returning in full circle
To declare the things he loved
As I too love the many things he loved
Because it is he who taught me to love them.

People who know me, say I have been lucky in having a poet for a father. I think it's more of a blessing, and carrying on his legacy is particularly dear to my heart, especially as I get older. I want him, and the historic and innovative role he played in shaping Modern Indian verse in English, to be remembered after his passing. I feel a responsibility to introduce him to younger poets writing in India today, and to overseas poets, whenever the opportunity presents itself. So, to answer this question, my poetic legacy comes with an amount of pride and humility, but also with great responsibility, and one that I take very seriously. I started writing poetry at the age of nine, as many children do, and later published some in the college magazine. I published my first book (*Family Sunday and other Poems*) in 1989, with a second edition in 1990. I was steeped in poetry from a very young age, having a poet for a father, and attended many poetry readings and art exhibitions with him, since he was also an art critic. He also held poetry reading sessions on how to read poetry out loud, something which I loved as a child, and the importance of which I emphasized to students in the teaching of poetry in my own classes. My favorite classes to teach were poetry and creative writing to high school students. During a long teaching career spanning a little over four decades, and raising two children while working full time, there was a hiatus in my writing. After semi-retirement a couple of years ago, I began writing again, kind of revived it, but with a new fervor.

The floodgates have opened,
The dam has burst,

> *The words pour out*
> *Like raging water, un-muddied and clear,*
> *Carrying everything in its path*

(from my poem. 'The Poetry of Homes')

Am I a poet? I write poetry, so I am a poet, but I will say I am evolving as a poet. I remain a work in progress.

I was in the process of getting my second book for publication, when my student and dear friend, Wendell Rodricks, one of India's top designers, passed away suddenly, a few months ago. His death was a shock. He had accepted my invitation to write the preface for my book. In deference to his memory, I have postponed the publication of the book.

In what ways do you think that your Jewish identity has influenced your writing?

I was born and raised in Bene Israel family in Bombay but my parents and grandparents were not orthodox Jews. We were liberal Jews. Here in Canada, they are known as Reformed Jews. I spent much of my childhood living with my grandparents, and an older aunt who taught me all the beliefs, customs and traditions of the Jewish faith. We were well assimilated into the Indian cultural milieu and readily accepted by peoples of all different religions and faiths. I went for the New Year prayers with my grandmother and aunt, but understood little, as the prayers were in Hebrew. My aunt had taught me to pray the *Shema*, and that was all the Hebrew I knew. I went to Christian schools and colleges and embraced Christianity. I loved the hymns of worship and the teachings of Christ as they gave meaning to my life. I particularly experienced a deep personal joy in that faith. My father, who was an open-minded and highly tolerant person taught me that all religions ultimately lead to the truth, just in different ways, along different paths. In the last few years, I have begun to explore my Jewish roots, something that happens to many individuals as they get older. It is an exciting journey. My poem 'Alibaug,' is the first poem I wrote that reflects my Jewish identity. Legend has it that the first Jews were shipwrecked off the coast of the Konkan, and the survivors went on to live in the neighboring villages. To quote from the poem:

> I miss Alibaug
> *The flickering lanterns, sleeping on mats, eating from *thalis*
> I miss Alibaug
> *The hushed whispers between cousins*
> *I don't know when I can return*
> *To the land of my ancestors*
> *The land of the Shanwartelis, the Oil pressers,*
> *I yearn for the unsullied rustic scenes,*
> *The dotted fields of cows and the music of their bells*
> *The hush of the chickens settling down for the night,*
> *And I don't know where the fish sleep*
> *In the folds of the waves*
> *Or in the folds of my memory.*

I have several others with Jewish themes, one that has particular significance for me. It is currently in publication. In boarding school, I was teased about "killing Christ", and wrote a poem called 'The Crucifixion,' in which I protested that I wasn't there when it happened, and in High School, I was called Shylock, though I was nothing like him. The nick name came out of the fact that we were studying Shakespeare's 'Merchant of Venice.' Both times, I was the only Jewish student in my class. These characters are just stereotypes, and as children mature, they begin to see beyond such unconscious prejudices.

We realize that you are multilingual and have taught English, French and Spanish in your teaching career. Do you feel that your poetry partakes of, and benefits from your multilingualism?

Yes, definitely, my poetry both partakes of, and benefits from, my multilingualism. I love reading Pablo Neruda and other poets in Spanish, and I do translate some of my own poems into French and Spanish, though I am conscious of the need to do this more consistently.

I have begun reading poetry in Marathi, especially the poetry of the well-known poet Shanta Shelke, with whom I had the privilege of working with in my first job at a college in Bombay (now, Mumbai), Marathi is the language we spoke at home, along with English. I love Hindi too, a love of that language was nurtured in me by a maternal aunt, who was a wonderful Hindi teacher. I wanted to major in English and Hindi in college, but that option was not available to me, so I took French, which I loved equally. My favorite subjects to teach in Canada were French and Spanish, both language and culture, to all levels of children. My belief is that poetry that is written in one's native language is more natural, in its ability to be powerfully expressive as it utilizes the natural idiom of one's identity. But with the myriad influences of so many languages, I often wonder "What language do I think in? What language do I dream in?"

A large number of critics opine that modern Indian English poetry started with your father. What do you think about it?

This has been a widely acknowledged fact, and I am humbled and proud to be the daughter of a man who dedicated his life to poetry, and to tirelessly mentoring so many younger poets and writers. He certainly was a foundational figure in this genre of writing and has been called 'The Father of Modern Indian Poetry in English.' Often times, he has been called 'The Big Daddy of Indian-English Poetry.' Whenever I visited him at the P.E.N office, there was a crowd of young writers clamoring for his attention and his advice, and I watched him poring over many of their manuscripts, late into the night, after a whole day of teaching, and his own writing. It was rough on my mother and us children. I get many messages about my father's contribution to the shaping of their poetry, and others speak of how his poems got them started on their own poetic journey. He especially paid great attention to detail, going so far as to advise poets on punctuation (commas and full-stops!) to achieve maximum impact in conveying meaning. He had a painstakingly incisive writing style. He was also the first to make the ordinary, the subjects of his poetry. Many writers followed suit. My husband recalls how, as a young man in 1975, he came across an article written by him for 'Freedom First' and marveled at how an Indian writer, writing in English, could express himself so beautifully, with economy in words, and hold the reader's attention. The critic Bruce King was foremost among several other critics, who paid tributes to my father as a pioneer and champion of Indian English poetry.

I am fiercely protective of his reputation as the Father of Modern Indian Poetry in English, because I personally witnessed first-hand his contribution to the field of poets writing in this genre of poetry. He put the needs of others before his own, often, actually always, setting aside the needs of his own family. It concerns me deeply when well established poets make him just a foot note in their interviews, or give him a passing reference, or express irritation about the significant input he had in giving them a head start in their poetic journeys of success. Often, he even edited huge manuscripts completed unrelated to poetry, charging nothing for his services. He was never interested in money or material things. It was complete dedication to writing and Literature. Anything I say on this subject will fall short in describing his historic role. The Journal of South Asian Literature of the University of Chicago dedicated an issue to my father, Nissim Ezekiel, in 1976. It is available to read online. I am in the process of writing a poem ('Waiting for Daddy') about my sentiments on the subject of his complete dedication to mentoring students, writers and poets. The poem begins:

> Daddy, the poets have gone home now
> They have taken their commas and full stops with them
> You must be hungry now, daddy
> Let's have lunch together,
> I have brought along my poem
> But it can wait
> I can wait.
> Eat slowly, take your time, enjoy your meal
> Let's laugh together
> At those silly 'knock knock' jokes
> You love to tell,
> Don't worry about the clever student
> Who will be waiting in the wings
> To ask you questions about your life
> And then ask others, who with masks of love
> Rob a man of his private suffering
> To indulge a world with its love of sensationalism.
> You took it to the grave
> We were splashed with the mud
> And they with false fame,
> How little it mattered to them,
> They who chose ignorance
> Of how we waited for you
> With our poems and our love
> And how it broke our hearts…

How do you read your father as a poet?
A copy of his Collected Poems is always on the desk, beside me, as I write. Among my father's poems, my favorite is 'Poet, Lover, Birdwatcher.' I read his poems daily, almost like a Devotional.

I have to say I greatly love, respect, and admire him as a poet, his honesty, rawness and vulnerability, his constant struggle for identity, his humanism, his love of nature and his search for the truth, his fearless admission of his flaws and his loneliness and the alienation that sometimes he sometimes felt from himself. I love that he was deeply rooted in his faith in God and mankind, without being maudlin or overtly religious, and had his roots firmly in India, and especially his love for the city of Bombay. In fact, he has often been called 'The Poet of Bombay.' It is easy to read his poetry and identify with so much of it, though it is profound, and contains layers of complex thought, simultaneously. I turn to his poetry for peace, for inspiration, for the economy and precision with which he uses his words, and for his depth of thought. I love that he made ordinary things the subjects of his poetry, and it has been said that he was one of the first poets to do so. He is a strong influence in my writing, and when I read my poems out to my husband, who is my best critic, and incidentally is a good writer himself, he often says, 'you sound like daddy.' I hear echoes of his voice in my poetry, though I have no illusions that I'll ever be a poet of his stature. I have a poem about that, again awaiting publication. What I will say though, is that though I have big shoes to fill (I have a brief poem titled 'Big Shoes to Fill'), I am walking with my father, every step of the way. I feel his loss palpably and struggle with the fact, that Alzheimer's disease ravaged his brilliant mind in his last years. He revised every poem meticulously, and was dedicated to his craft, and to promoting poetry in India. He had a strong work ethic and was a voracious reader. My father, Nissim Ezekiel, was a versatile poet and as a family, we were very excited when he won the Sahitya Academy award in 1983, and the Padma Shri award in 1988. He was a philanthropist at heart, and immediately donated the prize money from the Sahitya Academy award to charity. He also worked in an honorary capacity for the AJDC (the American Joint Distribution Centre), which helped less advantaged and poor Jews with their education. His work At the PEN India was also carried out in an honorary capacity.

Who were your father's favourite Indian poets?
I am not absolutely certain about his favorite Indian poets. I never discussed it with him, but he must have read poets like Rabindranath Tagore, Sarojini Naidu, Jayanta Mahapatra, Arvind Krishna Mehrotra, Toru Dutt, Mirza Ghalib, Henry Louis Vivian Derozio, T.K. Doraiaswamy and others. I think he must definitely have read Kabir, The Dhampadas, and Amrita Pritam. Of course, he read the poetry of all his contemporaries, and even published, and helped publish their poetry.

Do you remember the first volume of *Quest* edited by your father? Who were the poets featured?
I was too young to remember the first volume of *Quest*, though I knew my father was its first editor. The thing is I had 'lived life,' with my father. The analysis of his poetry and other writing was a subject for the scholars and the critics. It was founded in 1954 and some of the writers and poets featured were: Nirad Chaudhuri, Dilip Chitre, Allen Ginsberg, Jyotirmoy Datta, Mujibur Rehman, Agha Shahid Ali, Jayanta Mahapatra, Dom Moraes, Ashis Nandy, Gauri Deshpande, Adil Jussawalla, Mahapatra, A.K. Ramanujan, Saleem Peeradina, Arun Kolatkar, Dilip Chitre, Keki Daruwalla, Anita Desai, Kiran Nagarkar and Abraham Eraly.

You have been a witness to the formation of the canon of Indian English Poetry. What's your take on it?
There was clearly a phalanx of poets who formed the canon of Indian English poetry. I won't name them all here, but it seems to me that the heights they reached, still set the standard for excellence in poetry writing. (Of course, I feel that it must not become a rigid, unbending criterion, because poetry evolves over time and will reflect the mores of societal changes.)

I remember when I was very young and when my father was writing his poetry, it was P. Lal, who was himself a poet and an essayist, who gave a platform to Indian writers writing in English. In the 1950's, he founded the Writer's Workshop. I still have a memory, as a young girl, of the beautifully designed cloth-bound covers with Indian motifs, of the books of poetry that were published by him. Because they were attractive, they drew you to read them, and one was sure the contents must be excellent. (Talk about judging a book by its cover!). P Lal published writers like Pritish Nandy and Sasthi Brata, and later, Dom Moraes and my father, Nissim Ezekiel. However, any article I read about the subject reports that it was Nissim Ezekiel who 'created a voice and place for modern Indian poetry in English and championed the work of these poets'. My father also himself published a book of poetry by a fellow poet, and helped some struggling poetry magazines to survive, by financing them himself. I remember the conversations in my home about these undertakings, because he had a family to support, and a professor's salary does not really allow for business forays. My father's contemporaries were poets in India, like Jayanta Mahapatra, Gieve Patel, A. K. Ramanujan, Arun Kolatkar, Dilip Chitre, Arvind Krishna Mehrotra, Eunice De Souza, Kersi Katrak, P. Lal and Kamala Das.

Cricket and poetry, between the 1950s and 70s, were Bombay-centered. Do you recall those days?

Yes, I do! It was an exciting time and I recall the late 60s especially. During my school final exams, West Indies were playing India. I was glued to the radio, listening to the cricket commentary, rather than studying for the all-important ISC exams. That caused a lot of problems with my mother who despaired of getting me away from the radio. To her relief, I did well.

Truth be told, I wish I could tell you that, as a teenager in college in the 70s, I found great joy in the written (poetic) word. Instead, I found joy in the poetry of young love – its ecstasies and tragedies, changing every few months!!! I found joy in music, in friends, in eating out, in choirs, in rock bands and had memorized every song of the Beatles and the Mamas and the Papas and completed both my bachelor's and master's Degrees by 1975.

Who were the other important poets apart from your father at that time? Was there any significant event you can remember and would like to share with us?

The other important poets writing during my father's time were A.K. Ramanujan, Dom Moraes, Gieve Patel, Kamala Das, Arun Kolatkar, Jayanta Mahapatra, Arvind Krishna Mehrotra, Adil Jussawalla, Kersi Katrak, P.Lal, Dilip Chitre,and others.

I recall a time when I was doing the exams for my bachelor's degree in English literature, and there were two exams to write, in a day, with a short gap between. It was a time when I experienced severe personal stress, and I wanted to give up. The Bombay heat was excessive, and the material to be studied was vast. I had burned the midnight oil often and was exhausted physically. My father had a mantra for all such times in life. It was, 'if you are tired, don't quit, take a little rest and come back to it later, once you have rested.' He understood my fatigue, and told me that fellow poet, Kamala Das, had given him the key to her house, and as she would not be home at the time, I could go there, have my lunch, and get refreshed. He would walk me back to the examination Centre, a short distance away, to write my next exam. On every occasion, when I wanted to give up, whether it was a challenging job, or something else, he saw me through with his amazingly positive attitude. That was the only time he took away from others who clamored for his attention.

Your poems, we have observed, offer a grand wealth of nature imagery. Could you tell us about the images that attract you and how you put them to poetic use?

I love nature. It is a calming, healing force for me. The power of, and beauty in nature is unparalleled. I write about nature, naturally. The images in my poems are pictures of what I see, painted in words. I write about nature as I see it. I wish I were an artist. I would spend hours depicting the spectacular scenes I witness. I've done some sketches, sitting on my back patio, and I signed them, 'The Imperfect Artist.' Here, where I live, I am surrounded by nature. When I come downstairs in the morning to drink my first cup of chai, the scene that greets me is uplifting. I see the amazingly poetic clouds in a sky of changing colors, beautiful trees from the three kitchen windows, and the greenness of the freshly-mown lawn. My neighbor had planted five Lombardi Poplar trees in his backyard, and they have grown tall and stately now. They seem to speak to me. The neighbor across the alley has a large beautiful tree with some kind of red berries too, and we have two cherry trees, and an apple tree that we planted last year. It was a gift from my family for Mother's Day. Watching the robins bathing in the bird baths, the sparrows sitting in a line on the fence, 'the lilacs bending low over the fence,' and the colorful flowers in the front and back garden beds, the garden which my husband has lovingly planted (he's the one with the green thumb, my job is to water and weed), attracting the butterflies and some bees, soothes my soul. The squirrels chasing each other on the fence are fun to observe. We have winter six months of the year here, and summers are short. Some people find winter beautiful. I find it challenging, though I don't deny the beauty of the snow-capped mountains which can be seen in the distance, if you take a short walk and brave the slippery sidewalks.

I inherited the love of nature from my father. Our first rented home, a ground floor flat, had a large garden which the landlord zealously maintained, was chosen by my father himself. He always said he wanted to be buried in it. The flat was also close to the sea. We took regular walks with friends after school, and on Sundays with our family.

My father loved the sea breeze
He wanted to be buried in the garden
In our home by the sea
So he could feel the breeze on him
Under the earth,
He would be thankful for the coolness.

(from my poem, "The Many Things my Father Loved",
published in the May-June 2020 issue of *Muse India*).

My poem 'Family Sunday', published in my first book of poetry, describes this event. Father saw beauty in everything, a tiny blade of grass blowing in the wind, would be beautiful to him. As a young girl, I had to bend down real low to see its physical form, let alone appreciate its beauty. But now, on my walks, when I come across a blade of grass waving in the breeze, it presents itself to me with magical beauty, and I show it to my daughter, who looks puzzled! We have come full circle!

How have your roots in India and your routes that have taken you to different parts of the globe affected your work?
India is my birthplace, but the love of the country and Bombay (it is still difficult for me to say Mumbai), the city of my birth, flows very strongly in my veins. It is my home, not just physically, but emotionally and spiritually, and it's not mere nostalgia. It goes way deeper than that.

Tell Me If You Know Where Home Is
"All the lonely people, where do they all belong?'
Eleanor Rigby: The Beatles

I've never really left home
The place is always in my head, becoming as a noisy child's rattle,
If I shake my head from side to side

> *As Indians do back home, it still doesn't help,*
> *My ancestors often said 'Everything will be alright in the end*
> *And if it's not alright, it's not the end'*
> *I can't get away from the clamour of Indian sayings...*

(from my poem, "The Many Things my Father Loved",
published in the May-June 2020 issue of *Muse India*)

To describe my rootedness in India with a metaphor: the pine tree on my front lawn sends its roots so deep into the flower beds, making the soil too acidic for growing flowers. No matter how many of the roots we dig out, when we prepare the soil for planting, they stubbornly entrench themselves and seem to multiply! Similarly, my roots are too deeply entrenched, and I can't seem to uproot myself, though physically I have done that. However, home to me is also where my family is.

I took a year's sabbatical to pursue a Master's Degree in Education at the Oxford Brooke's University in England, and missed our home in the International School where I taught English, in the foothills of the Himalayas. I took comfort in the fact that we were going to return. But, now that we've immigrated to Canada, how do we return? That comfort of the assurance of return does not exist.

Indians have migrated to every part of the globe, and with this diaspora, Indian English poetry has reached the far corners of the world. The poetry that comes from diaspora Indians can be powerful in the context of memories, and the aching yearning for their homeland that they evoke in their writing. It is not mere nostalgia, as some like to think. They have lived in both places, and are richer for the experience. To provide an example, I am familiar with the poet Imtiaz Dharker, whom I knew as a young girl, since she was among the poets who formed part of the circle of poets with my father. My father himself lived for many years in England, and his first book of poems 'A Time to Change,' was published there. His poetry was definitely enriched by his experiences there, and his subsequent travels to myriad countries where he was invited to read his poetry and also as Writer in Residence and visiting professor. He always returned to India, and felt that if one went abroad to settle, one would be lost. My own experience confirms this as a fact, although I migrated for different reasons. Turning back was considered, but that posed many challenges, and did not happen. Reflections in hindsight are useful, only in so far as they help you move forward, and not leave you wallowing in regret. That would definitely be counterproductive. My father and I had many discussions about career paths. Again, I took that route for family reasons. One writer I admire is the novelist Jhumpa Lahiri. The richness of cross cultural experiences that find a voice in someone like her, is enriching. Diaspora writers carry two homes (or more!).

To quote again some lines from my recently published poem, 'Tell me if you know where Home is.'

I've never really left home
The place is always in my head
There are no cockroaches here, though not the reason for leaving
But I heard they are beginning to come to my city
Perhaps then I will feel at home,
We are becoming a bee city too, I can now plant flowers
That will bring butterflies, I chased them as a child,
in my home garden.

Still, if the cockroaches come, they will increase my homesickness
I had a fear of lizards too, been no sightings here yet
Home is anywhere the heart is, as the saying goes
With or without lizards and cockroaches,
Back home the bees are happy.

What are the themes that you are currently writing about? Tell us something about your work at present.

At present, I have been writing some Zen poetry. These poems are perhaps not in strictly Zen format, but more in theme. They are intended to be peaceful and contemplative in nature. In addition, I continue to work on poems that I began writing, but didn't quite finish for various reasons. One poem is called 'The Poet's Breath,' and describes how I was named. I enjoy writing poems about the art of poetry, and have written quite a few based on that theme. I think all poets write poems on this theme, at some point in their poetic career. I have recently written some 'Blessings' poems, and some on the Pandemic, one of which 'A Psalm of Hope,' has been published. I am in the process of preparing a talk entitled 'Authenticity and Simplicity' in the writing of poetry for college students in Jamshedpur, in India, which I have been invited to give, and an article about my father, for a newsletter put out by the International Organization of the Bene-Israel Jewish community, to which I belong. I was invited to do a Zoom presentation on my father by the Indian Jewish Heritage Centre, and the Cochin Jewish Heritage Centre in mid-May. The presentation was very well received. I write as I experience different events, and emotions related to those events, or scenes in nature I see unfolding around me. I live close to a lake and a nature reserve, and this affords me much pleasure and peace, in addition to superb flora and fauna. I write anecdotal poetry and all my poems tell a story. I have written a brief memoir of growing up Jewish in Bombay, seventeen pages to date, with the promise of more!

Can poets change society for good?

I'm going to answer this question with personal examples. But I would like to preface my comments by asserting my faith in the belief that poetry is good for the soul, and when the souls of human beings are touched and healed, soothed or moved,

Poetry has done its work. I place emphasis on the inner life, and at the risk of sounding clichéd, I'll say that when the souls of people change, society changes. 'Poetry is soul food'. Nature is pure poetry, yet also when poets write about nature, they can make us see aspects of it we may not previously have been aware of. We become conscious of the beauty around us and the value of caring for our environment. Children are taught to appreciate nature through poetry, and to write their own in response to things they love about nature.

Poetry addresses the inner life. When I get messages from people who have read my poetry, and respond to it by telling me that they not only enjoyed or 'loved' the poem, but could identify and relate with it in terms of situations they have been in, or that it helped them see something differently, or communicated emotions to them that they have been feeling, but have been unable to express, or brought about change in their way of thinking about certain ideas, I know that I have made a 'change for good', in my own small way. Poetry is therapeutic and definitely helps you to understand yourself and other people. There are poems written for different purposes, such as to bring about social change, poetry which influences social and political thought. For example, with the issue of racism that has resurfaced with the recent death of George Floyd, the poetry of protest is a powerful tool to not just express anger, but to bring about social change.

As mentioned earlier, poetry is very important for children. It helps them learn to use and love words to crystallize their thoughts and feelings. It helps them verbalize ideas and learn communication skills, so vital for their development. Children sometimes surprise us by writing the best poetry, unsullied by filters or the need to impress. They see the world with fresh eyes, and with wonderful innocence. I love reading poetry by children and also poetry written for children. Several months ago, I got a message, a sort of confession from one of my students in an

Introduction to Poetry course I was teaching at an international school. She apologized for passing a note to another student in the class in which she said, 'This is so boring.' She went on to say that she now writes poetry, and said she feels that 'she must thank me because she supposes I must have had something to do with it.' That message gave me joy and great hope for the future of poetry.

How, in your opinion, has the proliferation of online platforms given a boost to Poetry?
Undeniably, yes. At least in terms of the amount of content. The democratization which the internet has brought about gives voice to countless people who we would otherwise have never heard. It is not that people, in pre-social media times, did not have a love of poetry, or didn't write poems. They did. But their voice was never heard or was restricted by boundaries, never able to find publishers, or have something published which soon receded into the shadows, never found again or discovered accidentally. To quote those haunting lines from Thomas Gray's, Elegy Written in a Country Churchyard...

Full many a gem of purest ray serene
The dark unfathom'd caves of ocean bear
Full many a flower is born to blush unseen
And waste its sweetness on the desert air.

Who knows how many countless Shakespeares, or Kabirs, have gone on into obscurity, their works never to see the light of day? Perhaps, their works are treasured by immediate family, a loved one, but since unseen, never the general public. Today, we have a flood of poetry on numerous online sites. And variations in poetry. And people pushing boundaries in the way they interpret what poetry is. The imagery in the way words are arranged on a page, art, music and photography which add depth to plain words and carve their message indelibly on the reader's mind, add new paradigms of what we must now consider poetry. And each successive evolution becomes a welcome jolt!

Still, proliferation brings with it the enduring caution for 'buyer beware'! The mediocre jostle with the pure for attention and *"The race is not to the swift or the battle to the strong, nor does food come to the wise or wealth to the brilliant or favor to the learned; but time and chance happen to them all."* (Ecclesiastes 9:11, New International Version). Easily available content quantity does not always mean quality. Sometimes one feels, while reading, that publishing online becomes a race to the bottom with regard to quality. Poets may feel pressured with social media to publish more and more with quantity becoming the new currency of success. Acolytes indulge in flowery, excessive praise, inappropriate and completely out-of-proportion to the value of a poem. I too use online platforms, and I am conscious of the need to guard against the temptation to rush into print.

How do you look upon the travel of Indian English Poetry all these years?

As a child and well into my twenties, I recall that being 'good' at English poetry meant being well-versed in the poetry of England and the masters of American poetry. I don't think much has changed in that regard. Our curricula in school and university did not really include a body of Indian English verse, not in great depth anyway. Maybe the stray poem from Tagore and a passing mention of Sarojini Naidu. And, we as Indians, remain resolutely westward-looking in our quest for excellence in English poetry. Not that there's anything wrong with looking to the West... unless we are willing to concede that the downside of future generations of Indians doing the same and indulging in the same denial of Indian voices as worthy enough to be studied. If Rudyard Kipling, who is an Englishman, can be studied in India for his poems, so rooted in Indian culture, why not Indian poets?

My father's poem 'Night of the Scorpion' was included in school and college textbooks in India ad overseas and I observe that there is a trend toward some colleges including Indian poets in their syllabi.

What I see happening with Indian poetry is our Indian poets realizing that they do have their own voice. And it needn't be a clone of either England or Ireland or Wales or Scotland or America or Australia. We have Indian poets from myriad cultures, backgrounds, religions, native tongues in India and in diaspora-settled regions of the World who have voices in poetry, speaking in the one language all of them can understand (English). They have moved away from themes earlier thought to be real 'poetry' and opt instead for the poetry of their lived experiences. We have the great Rabindranath Tagore to look up to, to find inspiration in the literature, song and art of our own linguistic heritage and then express it in English. I see the same Indian-ness in my father's poetry, a refusal to be flowery, to dabble in fantastical imagery but instead write about the ordinary, the mundane – all deeply sourced in his lived, Indian experience.

Who are the poets from India and abroad whose work has motivated and influenced your writing?
The poets who have influenced and motivated me from abroad are numerous and I mention them in no particular order: Robert Frost, Emily Dickinson, D. H. Lawrence, Yeats, Wordsworth, Robert Browning, Keats, W. H. Auden, Maya Angelou, Gerard Manley Hopkins, William Carlos Williams, Edgar Allen Poe, Pablo Neruda, Octavio Paz, Charles Baudelaire, Victor Hugo, Paul Verlaine, the Israeli poet Yehuda Amichai, and my contemporary, the American poet Edward Hirsch, to name a few. Since I studied English and American Literature for my Bachelor's and Master's Degrees, I grew to love many of the poets who have a significant place in the history of the literature of their countries.

The poets from India are: Nissim Ezekiel, Rabindranath Tagore, Sarojini Naidu, Kamala Das, Gieve Patel, the Marathi poet Shanta Shelke, Ruskin Bond, and a few others. I am definitely making it a goal to try and read more Indian Poetry, particularly the poets that write in Marathi and Hindi, since I speak, read and write both these languages. The poets that write in the vernacular language are simply outstanding. Some of the languages I am not familiar with, I have to read in translation.

I must add a special note about the amazing poet Ruskin Bond who was a fellow resident of Mussoorie, in the northern Indian State of Uttar Pradesh. From 1982 to 1998, I taught in the English department of Woodstock International School. I was also a Career Counsellor for five years, after a sabbatical year at Oxford Brookes University, in Oxford England, where I obtained a Master's degree in Education. Ruskin Bond lived just a short distance away and we often met him on his walks in the local bazaar. On her sixth birthday, he granted a special interview to my daughter and autographed one of his books for her. She was absolutely delighted, of course!

Another amazing poet with whom my paths crossed was Shanta Shelke, the well- known Marathi poet. On completion of my Master's Degree from The University of Bombay, I got a job at a college where she was on the faculty. It was pure magic whenever she recited her poems to us.

And Nissim Ezekiel was an eloquent speaker, and could charm an audience with the way he recited his poems. I attended most of the readings, if not all, and was so proud to call him my father.

You also write short fiction. So, how do you build bridges between the two genres?
I mostly write stories about my father. They revolve around special memories of him, I had growing up, the things he said and did, and the things he taught me. One entitled 'Walt

Whitman and the Professor,' was published by *The Bombay Review*, a couple of issues ago. They would not strictly be classified as short fiction, but as nonfiction. I hope to publish a collection of these someday, again to preserve his legacy for my children and grandchildren. I have written one or two short stories, realistic fiction, like the one entitled 'Holi and Mary's Boy Child.'

I think poetry, fiction, and nonfiction are forms of writing that do not necessarily clash with one another. I don't feel a tension there. But I best express myself through poetry. It is a compact and condensed form of writing, though I have written longer poems as well. If I want to tell stories about the 'colorful and larger-than-life character' that my father was, I need the expansiveness that is afforded by prose writing. I have written some pieces about school memories, and other subjects such as happiness, and on the subject of arranged marriage. I was once on a panel discussion on this subject on All India Radio, Bombay.

What can be the role of a poet in the new normal times?
I'm certain that by now, most people are familiar with Kitty O' Meara's poem, '*And the People Stayed Home*", that went viral, and I'd like to begin with a few lines from the poem, which speak to the role of the poet in the new normal times. The poem starts with the activities we have all been almost forced into doing:

> *And people stayed home*
> *and read books and listened*
> *and rested and exercised*
> *and made art and played*
> *and learned new ways of being*
> *and stopped*
> *and listened deeper...*

The last stanza answers the question more specifically:

> *and when the danger ended*
> *and people found each other*
> *grieved for the dead people*
> *and they made new choices*
> *and dreamed of new visions*
> *and created new ways of life*
> *and healed the earth completely*
> *just as they were healed themselves.*

I myself have written poems and personal reflections, and my poem, 'A Psalm of Hope', believes that if you have been granted the gift of life, as in a new day, that there is hope. That is the role of the poet, to provide hope to himself or herself, and others. Here is a stanza from that poem:

> *The world will look different*
> *If you can spend a day*
> *Without fearful utterances of the words*
> *Virus, Pandemic, Lockdown,*
> *Not to deny their existence*
> *But render them voiceless and faceless*
> *For even a moment, so time may not pass you by.*

If my father were alive at this time, he would be reminding us about the resilience of the human spirit. I grew up with this teaching, and it has helped me tremendously in these trying and challenging times. In my home, all of us have made a conscious decision, not just to avoid mindlessly listening to depressing news, but to take each day a step at a time, and move forward, so as not to lose time, as my poem says. The virus is relegated to the background, though it forms the backdrop to our lives. It is a time for poets to provide hope, while recognizing suffering and death, caused by the Pandemic. It is a good time to be reminded to "Be still." I have been making a small list for myself about "The Things that I knew before the Pandemic, and the Things I learned from the New Normal." The profusion of poetry readings online, are testimony to the role poets play in bringing hope, cheer and goodwill to the world. I myself have participated in these readings. Poets have always influenced society, not simply by holding up a mirror to it, but by showing us how we can "improve our reflections." Those last words in quotation marks are mine, and affirm my faith in poets.

Is there a poem which reflects you? Can you please share this with us?

There are so many poems that reflect me…in fact all my poems are a reflection of me, so this is a tough choice. I'm sharing this particular one, since many of poems are about my father. He is mentioned either indirectly in them, or the poem is about him. I am still struggling with the loss of my father. I just don't seem to stop grieving for him. I had moved to another country, when I got the news that he was diagnosed with Alzheimer's in 1998. It was a devastating blow. My brother told me that it was better for me that I remembered him as he was before. He said he would not give me any news about him, as I was too far away. I last saw him in 1997. The poem 'Loss' is a Tandem poem, which means it is a poem written alongside one of my father's poems. It is a genre I have created, where I draw inspiration from a poem of his, kind of like a parallel poem, if you will. However, the subject, the imagery, and themes are my own.

Loss

Tandem Poem to accompany Poster poem 1 by Nissim Ezekiel
(My father talked too loudly…. but just before he died)
Dedicated to my father who sadly passed away
from Alzheimer's in 2004

My father could not talk to me
Before he died
Could not reach me in a distant land
Twinned in spirit, separated by geography,
I heard he remembered me
Said he could never forget me
Memory without a memory
Not able to remember
Not able to forget
Trapped in a maze of loss.
Two losses
The greater loss is mine

Thankfully,

He could not remember
What he had lost.

Thank you very much for this wonderful opportunity of interviewing you. We wish you rich creativity ahead and look forward to engaging with your work in future.

Thank you for the opportunity of sharing my thoughts and ideas with you.

(Published in *Flinders Journal*, volume 7, No 2, August 2020, from Australia)

Carrying her father's legacy,
Kavita is the extension of Nissim Ezekiel's soul.

https://www.differenttruths.com/interviews/carrying-her-fathers-legacy-kavita-is-the-extension-of-nissim-ezekiels-soul/

An interview with Urna Bose

You were the first born, the apple of your father's eyes. Help us, his fans and readers to see Nissim Ezekiel, an icon and the father of Indo-Anglian poetry through your eyes – the up, close and personal daughter's gaze. How was he, the loving, doting father? And the bond between the two of you?

Firstly, let me thank you for the invitation to an interview about my father, the late Nissim Ezekiel's contribution to Indo-Anglian Poetry. As his daughter, it is an honor and a privilege for me to speak about him. Preserving his legacy is a matter of not just pride, but also comes with a great responsibility, sometimes more important to me than my own writing.

"It doesn't matter who my father was; it matters who I remember he was". (Anne Sexton https://www.brainyquote.com/quotes/anne_sexton_131827)

To the world, my father was the poet, Nissim Ezekiel. To me, he would be the man I would call "Daddy" all my life. We do not choose the family into which we are born, but are placed there by, what some may, call Destiny or Fate, but by what I believe, is an all-knowing God, a God whose plans are perfect.

I heard from so many friends and relatives and of course repeatedly from my mother, that my father was delighted at my birth. He was a very fair-minded man and loved all his children equally, but being the first born, I was just a little more special to him, in the way that first-born children usually are. He did dote on me and was a truly indulgent father. We had a special bond as we both shared a passion for teaching, poetry, and life itself.

When I walked with him to the nearby store to buy a bottle of Vino Royale (the cheapest wine in those days), I would ask him what the occasion was, and he would reply, 'To celebrate Life!' We did not buy wine often, but when we did, he had a special spring in his step. My mother was puzzled at his kind of philosophy of life. She was a practical and down-to-earth person.

Due to family complications, I would live with him at my grandmother's house, from the age of ten, until I got married. It was difficult to be separated from my mother, though I saw her every Sunday, when she would spend the day with us, bringing goodies that my father and I loved. Living with my father, and caring for him and all his physical needs, deepened our bond. I would change the bed linen, tidy his clothes cupboard, dust, and organize the numerous books, and go shopping with him to buy those colored khadi kurtas he preferred to wear. The only thing he forbade me from doing was rearranging his writing desk. We joked that there was a sort of method in his madness. I was fortunate to be raised by my grandmother and another aunt. In fact, my grandmother's home, called "The Retreat," was the hub of the activities for her large extended family. I was raised by the proverbial 'village'. My father led such a busy and active literary life, would be out of the house from early morning till late night, so I was forced to share him with the world, often feeling lonely, despite loving aunts, uncles, cousins at my grandmother's home. I would wait for his '*Kavitam!*' on the creaky, old staircase at exactly 11 PM each night. We did, however, make several lunch appointments, visit the Jehangir Art Gallery together and I would attend most of his poetry readings, with my family. He was a delight to be with, a story-teller par excellence and had a wonderful sense of humor. Of course, the bonus came in the form of having him as a teacher at the University of Bombay when I was doing my Master's degree. When I taught morning college in my first job, he would insist on walking me to the bus stop at six-thirty in the morning, as I was overwhelmed by the construction workers that pushed and shoved their way in into the bus. Wearing a saree for work was mandatory, and it added to my woes! I had been threatening to leave the job when he said, 'Nobody leaves a job for a saree.' I later wrote a short Nonfiction piece with that title. The family situation was a challenging and traumatic time for me, and I have recently started expressing those experiences in my poetry. I have learned that in all circumstances, one does what one needs to, and the strength comes from faith in God, at least for me.

At the time of my birth, we lived at my grandmother's house, but it was for a short while only. We then moved as her home was getting overcrowded. My father selected our first home, a ground floor rented flat, not simply because it was near the sea, which he loved, but because it had a garden, and I could play in it. My mother would tell me that, and many other stories about his bond with me, growing up. She would often say that he spoilt me and would never say 'no' to me for anything. He was all for letting me have experiences, like going on the school trips to various parts of India, even though the cost strained the family budget. He would indulge my love of music by buying a Philip's turntable record player, which cost a fortune in those days. 'Don't worry,' he would say, 'the money will come'. He stole time from his sleep to write, after an entire day's teaching. When I wanted to go to boarding school at the age of nine, my mother was against the idea, but my father spoke his usual 'let her have the experience.' Later, knowing that I was part of the St Xavier's College choir that performed the Hallelujah Chorus at the Inter-collegiate choir competition (and won the trophy) and loved Handel's Messiah, he purchased the double album in Amsterdam, and carried it all the way, on the plane to Bombay. When he walked through the door with the white double album with the emblem of the gold cross on it, I asked why he did not put it in his suitcase. He said he was afraid it would break. On Saturday nights, there would a Quiz contest on the radio, with a question at the end, which I would answer. He would have a postcard ready in his meticulous handwriting, with the address provided, and literally walk briskly to the post box at the far end of our street to post it. I wanted to go with him, but he said, "you might slow the pace down and reduce your chances of winning the LP." Only the first to answer the question correctly would get the prize – an album from a popular band. I vividly remember winning an album of the group 'The Mamas and the Papas', whose songs I loved.

My father never told me what to do or what not to do, his guidance was always gentle and positive, but this day was different. I was off to St Xavier's College for my classes. I wore a lace white blouse with three red rose motifs on the front. My father looked up from the newspaper he was reading and asked me to go and change the blouse and wear something more modest. He said, "That kind of clothing will alienate the common man." I was surprised at his observation of the blouse, as I did not see anything wrong with it at the time, But I was respectful, and complied. Later, when I reflected on what he meant, it then became evident that travelling on a local bus, with people from quite a different strata of society, would invite unwelcome stares and comments. (But I took the blouse in my bag and changed into it in the college washroom – since St. Xavier's, in Bombay, was a very fashionable institution, the blouse would be 'all right'!!

The former Israeli President, Shimon Peres, was an admirer of Mahatma Gandhi, Jawaharlal Nehru and a supporter of India's bid on the UN Security Council. What is more, he had immense respect and love for Nissim Ezekiel's poetry. Peres often quoted from Ezekiel's poem *Acceptance* in his public lectures. Its opening lines, "I am alone/And you are alone. So why can't we be/alone together" was seen by Peres as a metaphor for how Israelis and Palestinians could sit across the table and discuss their common problems. Tell

us a little about this beautiful bond between Shimon Peres and Nissim Ezekiel?

First let me say how grateful I am to my cousin, Nissim Ezekiel, (my father's younger brother's son) for sharing the story of my father's connection with Shimon Peres. Without him, the story would never have been told.

The story behind the special connection between Shimon Peres and my father, is one of the highlights of my life, one that I will always treasure. My cousin, Nissim Ezekiel, (working at The World Bank at the time) who shares a name with my father, had gone to Israel for a meeting in 2005, as part of a team to assist the Government of Israel and the Palestinian Authority, in creating conditions for economic development in Gaza following the Israeli withdrawal. The meeting was led by Prime Minister Sharon. When Shimon Peres entered the room, he looked closely at the business cards of the delegates, and then asked, "Which one of you is Nissim Ezekiel, and are you related to the poet?" My cousin, who is an economist and a musician as well, replied that that the poet was his uncle, his father's older brother. Let me quote the exact lines, from my cousin's speech made in Las Vegas at the Adelson Educational Campus, titled: 'Honoring Shimon Peres' Legacy.' That is when Shimon Peres turned to him and said very simply, "You should know that your uncle is one of my favorite poets in the world, and when I need peace myself, I always turn to his poetry." Then, my cousin narrated in his speech how Mr. Peres went to his large, cluttered worktable (the resemblance to my father's desk struck me) and retrieved an older version of my father's poems. He proceeded to tell the team that whenever he met with his Palestinian counterparts in his endless search for peaceful solutions, he always quoted the lines from my father's poem 'Acceptance': "I am alone, you are alone, so why can't we be alone together." He used these lines in major public events, such as welcoming Jewish athletes from around the world to the Maccabiah Games in Israel.

When my cousin met Mr. Peres two months later he presented him with the latest version of my father's poetry, which had been published after his death. Later, he received a 'gracious' note from Mr. Peres on his formal letterhead as Vice Prime Minister thanking him for the gift of my father's poetry, acknowledging him as a remarkable poet and remembering his "Words of wisdom."

Nissim Ezekiel was awarded the Sahitya Akademi Award in 1983 for his collection, *Latter-Day Psalms*, and the Padma Shree five years later for his stellar, inimitable contribution to Indo-Anglian writing. Share with us an anecdote or two about the family's initial reactions and excitement, as and when the news started pouring in.

Each year, we returned to Bombay for a two-month vacation from the international school in Mussoorie, in north India, where my husband and I were working at the time. The residential school was closed for the winter months, and the students went home to their families. The Indian staff too went to their homes in different parts of India, and the foreign staff did some travelling, while others went to their homes overseas. Travelling by taxi down the winding roads from Mussoorie to Delhi, and then by the Rajdhani Express to Bombay with the children, was a much-anticipated event. From Bombay Central station we would go first to my mother's house for a couple of days. Little did we know how special the year 1988 would be!

One morning the bell rang at five am. We were all fast asleep, exhausted from our long journey. My husband stumbled to the door, to find a postman standing at the door with a telegram addressed to my father. My mother was already awake, frying the onions for the curry, as was her usual ritual. I do not recall whether she had heard the doorbell or not. In any case, my husband signed the receipt for the telegram and my mother asked him to open it. Suddenly, I heard an excited yell, 'Daddy has won the Padma Shri, daddy has won the Padma Shri.' I rushed to the living room and snatched the telegram from my husband's hands. All of this awoke my startled little children, who had no idea what the excitement was all about, and promptly returned to sleep. Later, the phone started ringing incessantly. My mother asked us to answer the telephone and said quite matter of factly, 'The meals still need to be cooked, even if daddy has won the Padma Shri,' she said. Friends and family kept calling all day long. We answered every phone call, completely unable to conceal our pure joy. I think Daddy only found out when I made a phone call to him at the PEN office. He remained blissfully unaware (as he mostly was of worldly happenings) of the commotion the news about him had caused.

Later that evening, daddy came home after his day's work. I started hugging him and crying. 'What's all the crying for,' he said in his characteristic calm manner. 'It's just an award.'

I don't remember much about where I was the day he won the Sahitya Academy award in 1983, but I do remember feeling immense pride in hearing the news. My father was a simple man with very few needs, never cared for money, awards, fame or prestige. He was devoted to his work with single-mindedness and simplicity, especially to poetry and to promoting the cause of poetry. He was a true philanthropist. If ever there was someone who could be described as "unworldly", it was him.

The archetype of a poet is his immense strength, suffering, and probably, a sense of guilt for the family. You are carrying Nissim Ezekiel's legacy. What are the symbolic cues and pointers about your chosen name, 'Kavita'? Was it destiny? Tell us how your father chose this evocative, "prophetic" name for you? Also, what does it mean to you and your poetry?

Preserving the legacy of my father is near and dear to my heart. As I mentioned earlier, it is not only accompanied by immense pride, but also carries with it a great responsibility.

A Beatles book of lyrics which he purchased for me one of his trips to New York had the inscription 'To Kavita, with faith in her potential.' It is taking me a lifetime to fulfil that potential, but I believe I have begun. On another occasion when he was overseas, he told me he had a photograph of me on his desk. The deeply personal words he spoke about what happened next are words I will cherish in the deepest part of my soul. He said that the photograph spoke to him and told him that I was the extension of his soul. The poems I write pay tribute to him, and, when they get published people can learn and understand the loving father and wonderful poet that he was. Most of my poems have a mention of my father, either directly or indirectly. It happens naturally as the result of the deep bond we shared. I have said in previous conversations that whatever shapes my life, shapes my poetry, and my father was a strong influence on my life in the life lessons he taught me. Whether he meant my name to shape my destiny, or destiny had a hand in bringing a prophecy to be, when I was born, there is certainly something uncannily powerful in the bond we shared.

Now to the question about my name. My father put a lot of thought into everything he did. I am glad he thought carefully about naming me. One's name is linked to one's identity. It is the first thing people ask when you are introduced to them. It can conjure up images in a person's mind of your character, though that may change when they get to know you. My name must have been symbolic to my father, if not prophetic. I am asked this question about the meaning of my name many times, which growing up I sort of took for granted, while still knowing that it was chosen with care. Kavita means 'poem' or 'poetry' in Hindi. My grandfather spoke Sanskrit, but I do not think that had anything to do with it. In Indian culture, children are named with meaning. This is more so than in Western cultures. In Hindu culture, the priest, after consulting the horoscope, comes up with a sound. The uncle then names the baby starting with the letter that corresponds to that sound.

My father could have chosen a Jewish name for me, but he chose Kavita, which makes me think it was meant to be intentionally symbolic. My mother and my siblings call me 'Kavi', which means 'poet', but that is just a nickname. They had no way of knowing that I may someday be a poet. Shakespeare said, "A rose by any other name would smell as sweet." I have often wondered if I had another name, would I have been a very different person?

My other siblings are also named with meaning, as I have named my children with meaning too.

In my opinion, there is some veracity in your statement about the archetype of a poet being his immense strength, suffering and probably a sense of guilt for the family. From my knowledge of reading and teaching poetry, I feel this largely applies to male poets, though I cannot provide the specific statistics. This is not to negate the fact that women writers possess strength, or that they suffer and carry the burden of guilt for the family. Perhaps women may tend to know more about how to achieve a balance between their passion for writing and their home life. Having said that, some women writers remain single out of choice, while others may end up divorced as the pull and tug of domestic life may overwhelm them. My father displayed immense strength in his resilience to challenging or adverse events. He always spoke of responding to tough circumstances by developing the right attitude to it. 'Happiness is a choice,' he maintained. All his life, he struggled with balancing his work with giving time to his family. It was particularly hard on my mother and us children too. He suffered from some of the choices he made as far as the family was concerned and we suffered a great deal with him too. All families have their issues, but when your father is a public figure, maintaining the privacy of the family life becomes an issue.

Tell us more about Nissim Ezekiel, the man and the poet. What would you say was his most interesting or memorable writing quirk? How much of your father is palpable in you?

It was interesting to watch how my father 'composed' a poem. I have described it in my poem 'How Daddy Wrote his Poetry.' He would lie down on the bed with a handkerchief over his eyes. The handkerchief features in my poem 'The Black Bicycle.' He had already lit a Menthol Cool cigarette and taken just a puff of it. The smoke from the cigarette would keep curling to the ceiling and die out. Then he would get up and write a few lines on a lined notepad, of which he had several on his cluttered desk. In the center of the desk was his typewriter, on which he typed his writing with two fingers. After writing a few lines of poetry, he would go back to the large old-styled bed and cover his eyes with his handkerchief once again. Then back to the desk, which I have described in a Haibun called 'The Poet's Desk.' When he was done, he would call me into the room, read out the poem, and ask me how I liked what he had written. He spoke slowly and deliberately and enunciated each word. He recited so beautifully, it put you in the exact mood that matched the theme of his poem. He accepted suggestions with that characteristic twinkle in his eyes, though it was not for me to know whether he made any changes based on my suggestions. After all, he was the Master poet!

So much of my father is palpable in me, tangible in a way that friends and family can recognize it. Whenever I did or said something to my mother, she remarked, "you really are daddy's daughter." When I was having an injection, I cried out for my daddy. My mother complained she had all the pain in giving birth to me, and I only screamed out for my father! Now, when I do or say something, or sometimes even when I write a poem, my husband will say, "that sounds just like your father", not just my colloquial use of language, but the spirit and the mood of things in which he would have expressed them. I have my distinctive style and am comfortable using my own voice. Some of the gifts my father bequeathed me are my appreciation and love of life, my passion for teaching, especially the love of the students in my classes, a love of literature, especially poetry, and my emphasis on the values of integrity, graciousness, and humility. Other important values he inculcated in me were a strong empathy with the suffering of others, compassion for the poor and the needy, and an attitude of live and let live. My father was the poet of the inner life, he said one must pay attention to the soul, and I have always given importance to this. My life is an expression of the things he poured into me.

Something else I inherited from him, is a complete lack of aptitude for numbers and figures. In other words, my math just does not add up and I have little financial acumen, much to the chagrin of my mother! My husband has reassured me that, despite the fact of being Jewish but not having their legendary business skills, everything I touch turns to gold. He says I have the Midas touch! I am certain that is an inheritance from my father. He gave away money to anyone who asked and sometimes even to those who did not. There was no calculation in his giving. All he saw was the need of the person in front of him. And he responded. His blessings have returned to me in full measure.

One of the disappointments of my life, and in my relationship with my father, was that he never once 'helped' me with my poetry. He felt strongly that he might be accused of nepotism and so, while he spent countless hours mentoring other young poets and writers, he studiously avoided reviewing my work. While my mother did not agree with his stance, I respected his choice, but I keep wondering whether the trajectory of my development as a poet and writer might have been on another plane altogether, had he taken an active interest in my work. He did, however, tell others that he was proud of me, and that I too was a 'poet'. He actually carried my first book to Israel and showed it to one of the organizers of the event he was speaking at. She later sent me a picture of the book he had given her.

(Published in *Different Truths* magazine, February 13, 2021)

Celebrating the life and vibrancy of India in its crowds

Yogesh Patel

Published on 20 Jan, 2022, 4:11 am, *iGlobal*

When one's father is a legendary poet who has defined the post-independence English Poetry of India, it is difficult for one to get away from the influence and poetics that he exerted.

Kavita Ezekiel Mendonca, someone of a great Indian Jewish heritage and poet Nissim Ezekiel's daughter, has faced that challenge diligently, sincerely, and by remaining loyal to the greatness of that poetry which defined India. It is the quality we would expect from a poet of her rare standing and context.

She doesn't struggle with this heritage but carves out her unique voice. In her poetry, we hear the noisy hustle and bustle of India, get a whiff of the aroma of typical dishes and cuddle up to warm people. It is the life we cannot find elsewhere on the earth. Now living in Canada, Kavita takes us to that nostalgia. Proudly, she is uncompromising about her love for India, as her father was when he tore into the Nobel Laureate Sir Vidya Naipaul's dismissive and ridiculing views of India expressed in his book, bursting with misplaced Anglophile superiority. So, Kavita doesn't disappoint us when she transports us to India we all know well.

Hence, when you read her poems, you realize she celebrates one distinct India where respect between communities is exemplary. This India, unfortunately, has been squandered by the Western Guardianists, but worst by the Indian intellectuals and artists abroad who have nothing good to say about India to please their peers. Against that backdrop, let us celebrate Kavita not only singing from "*Aamchi Mumbai*' (our Mumbai) but from "*Aamchi Bharat*" (our India*)*!

Kavita Ezekiel Mendonca has been a teacher of English, French and Spanish in colleges in India, and private schools overseas. She is a published poet, featured in various journals and anthologies, including 'The Journal of Indian Poetry in English' by Sahitya Akademi. Her debut collection *Family Sunday and other Poems* was published in 1989. Her chapbook *Light of the Sabbath* was published in September 2021.

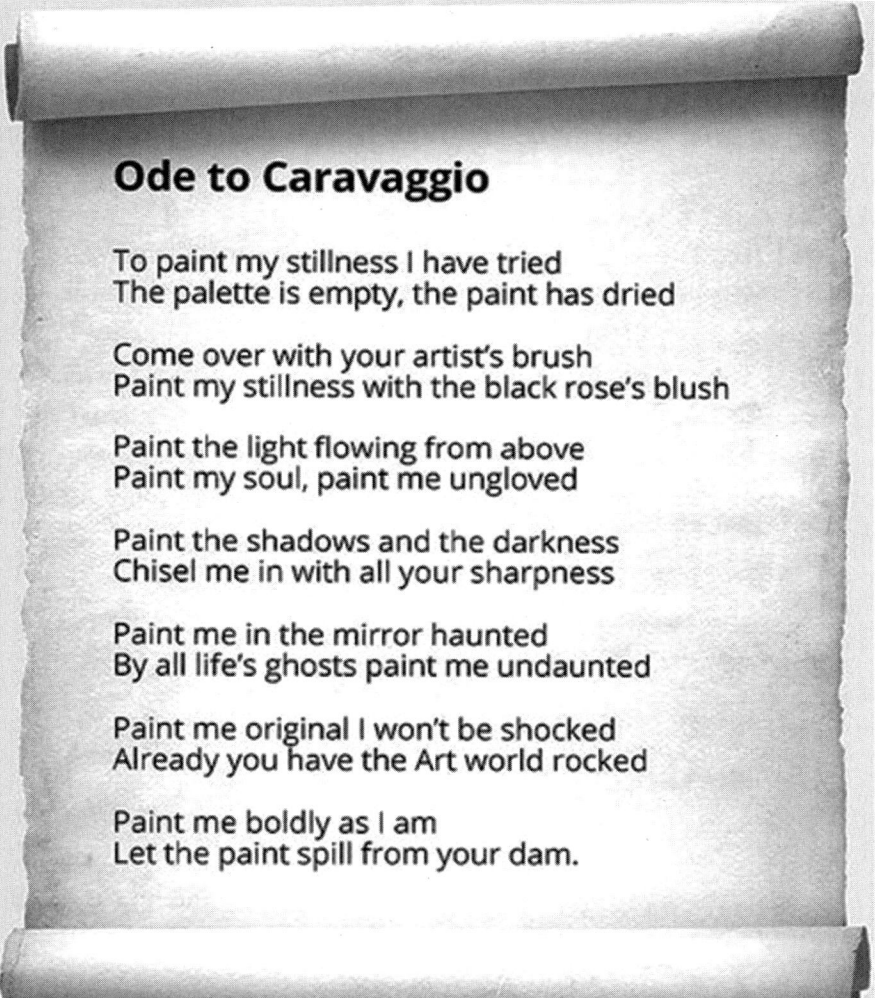

Ode to Caravaggio

To paint my stillness I have tried
The palette is empty, the paint has dried

Come over with your artist's brush
Paint my stillness with the black rose's blush

Paint the light flowing from above
Paint my soul, paint me ungloved

Paint the shadows and the darkness
Chisel me in with all your sharpness

Paint me in the mirror haunted
By all life's ghosts paint me undaunted

Paint me original I won't be shocked
Already you have the Art world rocked

Paint me boldly as I am
Let the paint spill from your dam.

About the lines above, Kavita says:
"The poem reflects my poetic craft, which, at its core, is about writing poetry that is being true to who I am, reflected in the last lines, which urge the artist to 'Paint me as I am'. The artist has total control of chiseling me with all his sharpness"

Q You cannot escape your father's legendary legacy to Indian English literature. Having been so close to him, how did you navigate your unique voice and style in poetry? Can you tell what his traits were in poetics? How yours stands out differently?

A To preserve the legacy of my father is near and dear to my heart. I have given several presentations about his life and his seminal role in Indian Poetry in English. As his daughter, it is an honor and a privilege to be able to do that. His *Collected Poems (1952-1988)* is like the Bible for me, always open on my desk for inspiration. He has set the bar high. It was not difficult to write poetry in my voice; since in my writing, I am able to be true to my own thoughts, feelings, ideas and experiences. As Shakespeare said in Hamlet:

> *This above all: to thine own self be true,*
> *And it must follow, as the night the day,*
> *Thou canst not then be false to any man.'*

My father wrote about ordinary things in a clear, direct manner. I write about ordinary things in the same vein. Often our tone is similar. My father was the poet of the 'inner self'. However, the depth and breadth of his poetic experiences are so vast, it is impossible to replicate. Whatever shapes my life shapes my poetry. His poetic journey was distinctively his.

Q The most inspiring stories of Indian integration are Parsees and Jews. As the Bene-Israeli Jewish community in Mumbai, how was your experience and response to sensitivities were different? Tell us how you have captured them to extract the universal values in your acclaimed poetry chapbook, *Light of The Sabbath*.

A Parsees and Jews blended quite seamlessly into the Indian environment. I grew up with a firm unity in my Jewish and Indian identities. There never was any conflict or tension between the two. When asked how I should describe myself, my father often said we were both Indian Jewish and Jewish Indian. A spirit of embracing the differences of the other communities around was natural. I did not even feel the differences. I had many Parsee friends and neighbors, and they, like us, followed their particular customs and traditions but participated in the religious festivals of the other faiths in India. I grew up in the Bombay of one world. In my chapbook, I have explored my Jewish roots through the warmth of the personalities that loved me growing up.

The other theme is the sacredness of light, which illuminates truths and realities beyond just the *sabbath* light. The light was a subject of conversation in my home – appreciating light in all the various forms of illumination that invigorated one's being.
It became something of sacred consciousness. In most faiths, light has a central role; for example, 'fire' represents light in addition to warmth and heat.

Q Your poems are a bright light of the Sabbath, a lesson in life, relationships, objects, and people. Pluralism, *bheed*, is India. But your *bheed* of images is vivid and bustling. Do you see your poems as salvage of the individual from the deluge of a crowd? What is the core message of your rich universe? Is Canada-your home now-still a peripheral space compared to your Indian inscape?
A For me, the individual is not lost in the *bheed*, but draws richness from it and contributes to it. I cannot imagine an India without its crowds and *bheed*. It is the crowds that give life and vibrancy to India, not that one does not need to get away to solitude of one's own! My universe is enriched by the memories of the individuals in my home and the wider, outer, colorful landscape in India. My roots are in India, and there is an inner ache at the core of my being which misses India and all things Indian. My home in Canada is where my family is and I'm

grateful for all the good things which my adopted country has offered and allowed me to contribute. It is not as though I have not struggled to slough off 'India' in my being. As I expressed it in my poem *"Tell Me If You Know Where Home Is"*:

I've never really left home
The place is always in my head, becoming as a noisy child's rattle,
If I shake my head from side to side
As Indians do back home, it still doesn't help...

Usha Kishore in conversation with Kavita Ezekiel

Usha Kishore (UK): Shalom Kavita, I am delighted to be able to speak to you about your esteemed father, the late Nissim Ezekiel and his work.
Kavita Ezekiel (KE): Thank you Usha. It is a pleasure to speak with you about my late father's work.

UK: Let me begin with Indian Jews. The Indian Jewish identity cannot be considered in a western context. The American Jewish author Nathan Katz[1] feels that Jewish history is at its happiest in India as there has been no religious persecution, unlike Europe and elsewhere in the world. What do you feel?
KE: Growing up, I never experienced any kind of religious persecution. I was never conscious of being Jewish as something separate from the rest of India. We mingled freely with everyone – Muslims, Christians, Parsees, Anglo-Indians, and Hindus. I always felt that people were very interested in my Jewish heritage. About the only time I remember being judged for being Jewish was in school when we were studying *The Merchant of Venice*, when classmates teased me and called me 'Shylock.' Also, at boarding school, when I was nine years old, I was accused of 'killing Christ' and I wrote a poem called 'The Crucifixion'. I take this to be the consequence of stereotypes engendered through literature. And studying the Bible at a Christian school, exerted a strong influence on children to stigmatize the only Jewish student in the classroom. Looking back, I now realize that it was childish ignorance, but at the time, it was hurtful and insensitive. Ironically, I had a similar experience to the one my father describes in the poem, 'Background, Casually,' except I attended a school run by Protestant Christian missionaries.

> *I went to Roman Catholic School*
> *A mugging Jew among the wolves.*
> *They told me I had killed the Christ.*
> *('Background, Casually')*

The distinctive experience of Jews was that they were held in high esteem and never faced discrimination in India. In the later part of the 18th Century, many Bene Israelis moved to Bombay (Mumbai), Ahmedabad, Karachi and Calcutta and distinguished themselves in fields such as Education, Law and the Armed Forces, including the British Army's 'Native Forces', and its successor, the Indian Army. Ezekiel highlights his ancestry in the most defining poem of his life, 'Background, Casually':

> *One among them fought and taught*
> *A Major bearing British arms.*
> *He told my father sad stories*
> *Of the Boer War...*

UK: Nathan Katz opines that the Indian Jewish identity is created by the community's interaction with the Hindus and other Indian religions. Do you agree with this?

KE: I don't know if the Indian Jewish identity is created exclusively by the community's interaction with the Hindus and other Indian religions. They had a pretty strong sense of their own identity. Certainly, the close relationship with the Hindus might have influenced their identity and was largely because the Bene Israeli Jews blended seamlessly into the cultural milieu, while retaining their own customs and traditions. They spoke Marathi alongside English, ate Indian foods, the women wore sarees, and did not experience any anti-Semitism. Prayers were recited in Hebrew, and regular visits to the synagogue on festival days was part of their cultural identity. They were accepted by the Hindus with all these traditions. The Bene Israeli Jews inter-married with Catholics, Parsees and Muslims as well. Whenever I had asked my father whether we were 'Jewish Indian' or 'Indian Jewish', he had always replied 'Both'!

UK: I feel that Ezekiel does not explore the cultural mechanisms that define India's diverse Jewish identities, but he responds to the changing cultural and political atmosphere of Independent India. Do you agree?

KE: While he was conscious and aware of the diverse Jewish identities in India, the dominant themes in his poetry and writings were mainly concerned with India and 'Indianness.' I don't think that the political changes or atmosphere of 'independent India' necessarily took centre stage in his poetry. He was immersed in the experience of being human, of change, of his own inner struggles, but wrote as an observer, detached from the experience.

UK: Do you think that Ezekiel's poetry addresses the minority status of the Indian Jews and their exodus from India and also provides a dialogic response to Hinduism?

KE: He was aware of the exodus of Indian Jews, but he does not write about it. I remember him clearly saying about the desire of Indians to emigrate 'west' to 'make it.' I quote him: 'Who will remain to do something for India?' There is no 'dialogic response' to any faith. The writing of poetry was central to his life. He always taught me that the important truths of life are expressed in all religions, be it Hinduism, Islam, Judaism or Christianity. My father was also widely read in the sacred texts of all religions and interested in different ways of approaching the search for truth. He chose to remain in India, a country he loved deeply, as do I, and our family did not emigrate to Israel.

I have made my commitments now.
This is one: to stay where I am,
As others choose to give themselves
In some remote and backward place.
My backward place is where I am.
('Background, Casually')

UK: How does Ezekiel's poetry reflect on his Jewish identity? Do the issues of identity and alienation figure in his work?

KE: There is no overt 'Jewish identity' which emerges as a theme anywhere in Nissim Ezekiel's poetry. No doubt, being born Jewish influenced his use of language and the feeling that the man is actually praying to his God in many of his poems. Irrespective of religion, anyone could relate to those 'prayers'. It does not mean that the sentiments expressed e.g. in *Latter Day Psalms*, are in any exclsusive sense 'Jewish'. At the end of *The Latter Day Psalms*, he does say "Now I am through with the Psalms/they are part of my flesh. "Much later in life, towards the end, Ezekiel began to read the Kabbalah (Jewish mysticism). But I recall that his interests in religious texts were eclectic, not driven by religious sentiment, but the keen inquiry of an avid learner, devoid of any pre-judgement. In his poem 'Jewish Wedding in Bombay', he mentions that his father:

... himself had drifted into the liberal
creed but without much conviction, taking us all with him.
My mother was very proud of being 'progressive.'

UK: Can the poem, 'Background Casually', be considered the poetic autobiography of Ezekiel, highlighting the issues of identity and alienation, nationality and marginality?

KE: The poem is clearly autobiographical and the themes you mention do occur naturally, since they were an integral part of the poet's experiences. Ezekiel outlines his struggle for personal identity, as he tries to socialize with students from diverse faiths in school. He is also bullied by the boys from different faiths as he describes it 'a mugging Jew among the wolves'. The search for identity continues:

> *At home on Friday night the prayers*
> *Were said. My morals had declined.*
> *I heard of Yoga and of Zen.*
> *Could I, perhaps be rabbi-saint?*
> *The more I searched, the less I found.*

However, Ezekiel has always identified himself with India and felt completely at home there. There was no conflict with a search for nationality. Many poems speak of his Indianness. I don't think he ever felt marginalized. Ezekiel was a natural outsider, being born Jewish, but an insider, as he loved his country, and particularly the city he was born and raised in, which was Bombay. He highlights this in Poster Poems':

> *I've never been a refugee*
> *Except of the spirit,*
> *A loved and troubled country*
> *Which is my home and enemy.*

UK: The poem 'Background Casually' refers to: *My ancestors among the castes/ Were aliens crushing seed for bread/ (The hooded bullock made his rounds)*. Am I right in thinking that this is the reference to Ezekiel's cultural connections and the *Shanwarteli* community?

KE: Yes, you are right; the quote is a reference to the Bene Israeli community, who were oil-pressers. The reference to 'aliens' signifies that they clearly were outsiders to the local community. The term 'Bene-Israel' refers to the largest of the three Jewish communities in India (the other two are Cochin and Bagdhadi Jews). According to legend, they descended from 'seven couples' who were the remnants of a shipwreck near the village of Navgaon, on the Konkan coast in India, near Mumbai. Because of the centrality of the Prophet Elijah in their oral traditions, their ancestors may have lived in the time of Elijah in Israel and their arrival in India dates anywhere between the 8th century BCE and 6th century AD. They became assimilated in the coastal communities, taking up farming, carpentry and mainly, oil pressing. Because they observed the Jewish Sabbath and did not work on Saturdays, they came to be known as 'Shanwar Telis' or 'Saturday Oil Pressers'. Today, the Bene Israeli number about 5000 in India and 40,000 in Israel, after an exodus of Jews from India in the 1950 and 60s.

UK: How does your work as a poet reflect your Jewish identity?

KE: Several of my poems in the last few years are based on Jewish themes. As I grow older, I have also begun to explore my Jewish roots, and my poetry is an attempt to come to terms with my cultural heritage. The poems are influenced less by me being religiously Jewish, and more by the memories of growing up in a Jewish home, with all its rituals, traditions, beliefs, festivals. At the Christian school, I attended, I learned much from the Bible with a focus on the New Testament. A couple of my poems, like 'Alibaug' and 'Miracles' have Christian references. 'Alibaug' is a poem with a specifically Jewish theme, set in the then-predominantly-Jewish village of my childhood, where my uncle owned a grain mill. Alibaug has changed much now, with all the rich people buying homes there, and the hotels that have sprung up.

I think a good portion of the Jewish prayers being in Hebrew made it difficult for me and could have contributed to my lack of knowledge of the essence of Judaism. In recent years, I have been deeply affected by the Holocaust – reading about the persecution of Jews, their suffering and the senseless slaughter of 6 million people.

Several of my poems over the last few years are based on Jewish themes as a reflection of my exploration of my Jewish roots and cultural heritage. The poem 'Alibaug', is one example.

> *I miss Alibaug*
> *I don't know when I can return*
> *To the land of my ancestors*
> *The land of the* Shanwartelis, *the Oil pressers*

Having attended a Christian-missionary school in Bombay, the teachings of Jesus were a strong influence on my life. The poem 'Alibaug', makes reference to a story I loved.

> *I had heard of Jesus in school*
> *Of how He walked on water*
> *And His command to still the storm,*
> *I remember praying to have that kind of faith*

My poems 'I Still sing The Shema' and 'Light of the Sabbath', based on Jewish themes have been recently published in *Indian Literature* and *Harbinger Asylum*. Here are a few lines from each of them:

> ### I Still sing The Shema
> *I watch movies about the Holocaust I cannot bear to watch;*
> *I become an enraged bull*
> *I leave the room and re-enter like the Matador*
> *determined to conquer the beast*
> *I wish I had The Matador's nerve and skill.*

Light of the Sabbath

Each Friday evening, we squeezed
The purple grapes of Faith
And each Saturday she read
All one hundred and fifty Psalms

UK: How has your father's work influenced your poetry?

KE: My father's work has influenced my poetry in a sort of unconscious way. I had 'lived life with him,' so many of the ideas, values, and attitudes to life he passed on to me, find expression in my poems. Of course, the style and format of my poetry is different. I have my own voice, and am so glad to have discovered it, and am continuing to hone my craft. So many of the themes I write about, for example the theme of nature, have been influenced by my father. Every poem I write makes either a direct or indirect reference to him. Of course, being raised by him, deep down in my subconscious mind, things surface, and get written into the poetry. Both of us use a more direct and colloquial style and write a great deal about ordinary things. Whatever shapes my life, shapes my poetry, and of course that has been the same for him, as for all poets. My father has played such an important role in my life that of course things he taught me are a permanent part of my psyche. He was a true intellectual, though. I have never tried to imitate him, nor do I feel like I am walking in his shadow. Rather, I know that I am walking alongside him, sharing space with him in the world of poetry, if ever so slightly. It is amazing and humbling to have a poet of his stature as a father. He always spoke of his faith in my potential, and my hope is to fulfil that potential, and preserve his legacy. which is more important to me, in many ways, than my own writing.

Suppose I were a Shooting Star
I would want to be seen
That would be my only meaning
What is there after all
In shooting across the sky
And being burnt up...

('The Eternal Ego Speaks', from Ezekiel's Poster Poems)

My father loved the stars
There was a surge in the twinkle in his eyes
Like a gently rising ocean tide
When he spoke of the stars,
Shooting stars were his favorite...

(From 'The Many Things My Father Loved 'by Kavita Ezekiel
Mendonca)

UK: Kavita, Thank you very much for this enlightening interview. Your father will always be remembered for his eclectic verse and his dynamic poetic sensibility. Best Wishes with your writing and future poetry collections.

KE: Thank you Usha. I have enjoyed this conversation with you.

Notes:
Nathan Katz, *Who are the Jews of India?* (California: University of California Press, 2000).

Published in Indian Literature (New Delhi: Sahitya Akademi, July / August 2020)

Harbinger Asylum (Fall Issue, 2020)

An excerpt from Kavita's memoir, about Jewishness, has recently been published in the October issue of SETU magazine https://www.setumag.com/2020/09/banana-lane-childhood-memoir.html

(Published in Muse India, March-April 2021 Issue)

CONTRIBUTORS

Adil Jussawalla, poet and critic, is one of the most well-known and influential voices in Modern Indian poetry in English. He was the founder of a small independent press called Clearing House. He was named poet laureate of the Tata Literature Live Festival held in Mumbai in 2021.

Alan Mendonca, Nissim Ezekiel's son-in -law, is married to his eldest daughter Kavita. He is a consultant and Senior Project Manager by profession.

Elkana Ezekiel, Nissim Ezekiel's son, is the youngest of the three children. He has worked as Marketing Director for multinational companies, as a CEO for a pharma company, and is currently Adjunct Professor of Management at a Management Institute in India.

Fiona Fernandez, a feature editor at Mid-day magazine in Mumbai, is a well-known journalist and author.

Gayatri Mazumdar is a poet, writer and publisher. She is the founder-editor of *The Brown Critique*. She worked with Nissim Ezekiel at the PEN office in Mumbai for three years.

Gieve Patel is a well-known Indian poet, playwright, painter, and physician. He was named poet laureate at the Tata Literature Live Festival in 2022. His first book of poems was published by Nissim Ezekiel.

Jeet Thayil is an Indian poet, novelist, musician, and editor. He has also worked as a journalist. He has numerous significant awards and prizes.

Kamal Balsara-Bacha was a student in Kavita Ezekiel Mendonca's Advanced Placement English class at Woodstock International School in North India. She is currently teaching English at a school in Mumbai.

Menka Shivdasani is a well-known poet, editor, journalist, and author. She is the Mumbai coordinator of the global movement, 100 Thousand Poets for Change, and has recently taken on the role of co-chair at Asia-Pacific Writers and Translators Association. In 1986, she played an important role in founding the Poetry Circle in Mumbai.

Mohana Rao was a student of Kavita Ezekiel Mendonca at the Woodstock International school in North India. She is one of the "two Stars" of Nissim Ezekiel's poem 'Lost and Found in Mussoorie.'

Olinda Belt was a student of Kavita Ezekiel Mendonca at the Woodstock International school in North India. She is one of the "two Stars" of Nissim Ezekiel's poem 'Lost and Found in Mussoorie.'

Raul da Gama Rose is a poet and music critic. He was a founding member of the publishing house "New Ground," in Bombay and published significant poets like Eunice De Souza. He is also a founding member of Jazz Global Media, along with Mr. Navas.

Saleem Peeradina was a distinguished poet, writer, editor and teacher. He founded the Sophia Open Classroom in Bombay in the 70s. Saleem lived and taught in Michigan.

Salil Tripathi is an Indian journalist, editor and author. He is the Chair of the PEN International Writers in Prison Committee. His writing has appeared in prestigious magazines like *The New Yorker*.

Shalva Weil is a Senior Researcher at the Seymour Fox School of Education at the Hebrew University in Jerusalem. She is a renowned author and specializes in research in the area of Jewish identities of ethnic Jewish communities in various parts of the world.

Shanta Acharya is a poet and novelist and lives and writes in the U.K. She won a scholarship to Oxford and was one of the first batch of women to be admitted to Worcester college in 1979.

Subodh Deshpande is a Brand Consultant by profession and a published poet.

Sudeep Sen is a celebrated Indian poet. He has published several books of poetry and edited many important anthologies.

Sujatha Mathai published several collections of poetry, making an important contribution to the field of Kerala poetry in English – and, thereby, of modern Indian poetry in English.

Pippa Rann Books
and
Global Resilience Publishing
(imprints of **Salt Desert Media Group Ltd., U.K.)**
Working in collaboration with international distributors
from the whole of the English-speaking world.

Salt Desert Media Group Ltd. (est. 2019) is a member of the Independent Publishers Guild.

At present, the company has two imprints, **Global Resilience Publishing** and **Pippa Rann Books (PRB).**

PRB was launched on August the 17th, 2020, with the first title published in Autumn 2020 – Avay Shukla's *PolyTicks, DeMocKrazy & MumboJumbo: Babus, Mantris and Netas (Un) Making Our Nation.*

Since then, our publications include prize-winners and best-sellers, and with books with introductions by eminent people such as Shashi Tharoor, the Pope, and the Dalai Lama.

Pippa Rann Books focuses entirely and exclusively on publishing material that nurtures, among Indians as well as among others who love India, the values of democracy, justice, liberty, equality, and fraternity.

That means we publish:

• Books and media by **authors of Indian origin**, on any subject that broadly serves the purpose mentioned above.
• Books and media **by non-Indians** on any subject connected with India or with the Indian diaspora, which serves the purpose mentioned above - again, broadly interpreted.

* * *

By contrast with PRB, Global Resilience Publishing began operations in Autumn 2021, with the first publications being released from Summer 2022. As the name suggests, the imprint focuses on subjects such as:

- Coping with the impact of climate change
- The Global Financial System
- Multilateral Governance (e.g., the United Nations)
- International Corporate Governance
- Leadership around the World
- Family Firms around the World
- Global Values
- Global Philanthropy
- Lobbying
- Commercial Sponsorship
- New Technologies, including AI, Gaming, VR, & ChatGPT.

Two things make GRP unique as an imprint:

1. Our books take a global perspective (not the perspective of a particular nation);
2. GRP focuses exclusively on such global challenges.

* * *

Global Resilience Publishing and **Pippa Rann Books & Media** are only two of several imprints that are conceived of, and will be launched, God willing, by Salt Desert Media Group Ltd., U. K. The imprints will cover different regions of the globe, different themes, and so on. And if you have an idea for a new imprint that you would like to establish, please get in touch.

Prabhu Guptara, the Publisher of Salt Desert Media Group, says, "For all our imprints, and for the attainment of our incredibly high vision, we need your support. Whatever your gifts and abilities, you are welcome to support us with the most precious gift of your time. The *seva* you do is not for us but is for the sake of our nation, and for the world as a whole. Please email me with your email, location, and phone contact details on *publisher@pipparannbooks.com*, letting me know what you feel you can do. Could you be an organiser or greeter at our events? Could you ring people on our behalf? Write to people? Write guest blogs or articles? Write a regular column? Do interviews? Help with electronic media, social media, or general marketing? Connect us with people you know who might be willing to help in some way or other?"

He adds, "I am one man, so I do not and cannot keep up with everything that is happening in India, let alone in the world. There are many challenges and numerous opportunities – help me to understand what these are. Pass information on to me that could be useful to me. Put your ideas to me. Any and all insights from you are most welcome, as they will multiply our joint effectiveness. It is only as we work together that we can contribute effectively to changing our nation and our world for the better".

* * *

Join our mailing list to discover books
which will inform you on a wide range of topics,
and inspire you as well as equip you.

www.pipparannbooks.com

PHOTOGRAPHS

The Ezekiels: My father, Nissim Ezekiel, back row, centre.

My maternal grandparents, Isaac and Leah Jacob.

Wedding picture of my parents,
Nissim and Daisy Ezekiel
(Bombay, 1952)

My mother, Daisy Ezekiel.

Nissim Ezekiel's sisters, Asha (left) and Sarah right), with their
husbands, Atmaram Bhende (left) and Srinivas Rao (right).

Baby Kavita

Sisters… Kalpana (left) and Kavita.

My mother, Daisy and I (Kavita).

My paternal grandmother, Diana,
holding me (Kavita) and cousin,
Nissim, standing.

My father (center) at a function at my grandmother's school in Bombay, with my sister Kalpana to his left and I, to his right.

My father with all three of his children in Goa.

Kavita and Alan (newlyweds)
with Kavita's mother and brother, Elkana, in Panchgani 1980.

My father holding my sister Kalpana, and me sitting between my mother and father. The picture was taken outside my home in Bombay

My paternal grandmother, Diana, with me, Kavita, on the right and my sister Kalpana on the left.

My father and mother with my sister and my brother
outside our home in Bombay.

At our home in Bombay, my sister Kalpana (standing)
and me seated by the door.

Kavita in Bombay, 1979

Wedding picture of Alan & Kavita
Mendonca, with Nissim Ezekiel
in the background.

My sister Kalpana to the left, my brother Elkana in the center, and me,
Kavita, on the right.

Kavita with her mother, Daisy, in Bombay in the 1990s.

Kavita on a walk with her brother, Elkana, in Calgary, 2015.

המשנה לראש הממשלה
VICE PRIME MINISTER

August 14, 2005

Mr Nissim Ezekiel
125 Pihaa Street
Lahaina
Hawaii (HI) 96761
U.S.A.

Dear Mr. Ezekiel,

Thank you so much for sending me the second edition of your uncle's collected poems which I shall, I have no doubt, savour with much pleasure.

Nissim Ezekiel is indeed a poet I admire, and I am happy that his words of wisdom, and his vision, will be shared by the public at large, thus serving to perpetuate the memory of a remarkable poet in a most appropriate manner.

With all good wishes,

Sincerely yours,

Shimon Peres

Letter from Shimon Peres to my cousin (Nissim Ezekiel, Jr.)
on receiving my father's Collected Poems as a gift.

Shimon Peres with my father's book (Collected Poems) open, reading the note
which my cousin, Nissim Ezekiel Jr. wrote to him.

The Second Candle
What's the second candle for, I asked
my wife that Friday night. Wait, she said,
till they are lit and the prayer is over.
Then she turned to me with a cunning smile:
The first candle is for God's daily blessings,
just the usual things, you know,
Life itself, food and drink, love, children,
Friends, relatives, books, flowers,
freedom from misfortunes,
all the plain prose of daily breath
which, for me, is poetry. She paused,
wanting me to repeat the question
what's the second candle for?
I didn't repeat it, patiently silent...
Then she added quickly before turning away.
The second candle is for a miracle I need
a special favour, a certain turn of events
what work alone will never bring,
a gift we do not quite deserve
but still may get by asking for it.
Call it grace, if you like, a windfall,
bonus, dearness allowance,
more than a promotion,
Some kind of new dimension, revelation.
Well, that's what the second candle's for.
Now do you understand.
She didn't wait for my answer.
I looked at the two candles shining there
and wondered at the faith
that deals so simply with its God.

The poem was composed, inspired by a request from my mother who wished to light a second candle on the Sabbath, to pray for a miracle for the failing eyesight of one of her sisters. In the last lines my father 'wondered' at my mother's faith 'that deals so simply with its God.'